Now It B

by Gary Markwick

Published by

PUBLISHING

i2i Publishing. Manchester.
www.i2ipublishing.co.uk

Cover designed by Denize Churnin and Palamedes PR

ISBN 978-0-9567668-8-5

Now It Begins

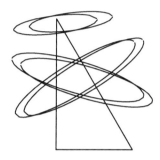

by Gary Markwick

Now It Begins

Always give with love and compassion

*Without guilt, bitterness or an empty
feeling*

Open your hearts to those who suffer

*And show forgiveness and
understanding*

To a world which needs healing

This book is dedicated to my
stepbrother Leon Misell
Who had great awareness, understanding
And a thirst for knowledge

07/11/1973 – 18/02/2012

Now ItBegins

I would like to give special thanks to my lifetime partner and friend, Denize, who has helped me with the writing of this book.

Without her all this would not have been possible.

I would also like to say thank you to Brenda who has been an amazing asset in correcting and putting together this book. Bless you.

This book is also dedicated to friends and family and the lost souls of this world, in the hope they may find peace and understanding within themselves and for others in these changing times.

About The Author

Gary Markwick (Diploma of Hypnotherapy, NLP) is an international palmist, psychic, a Usui and Karuna Reiki Master Teacher and spiritual healer. Gary is also a qualified clinical Hypnotherapist, a Past Life Regressionist and has written a course on the Law of Attraction. He runs his own workshops on the Law of Attraction, as well as on Reiki.

Gary has been a professional palmist and psychic for around 20 years and has read the hands of thousands of people from around the world, including some celebrities. Gary has appeared on Sky TV and BBC Radio 4 and has had coverage in newspapers, including his reading of a handprint for a national newspaper, of Barack Obama, before the US Presidential election.

In his capacity as a talented singer and songwriter, Gary has performed at venues such as the UK's Glastonbury music festival with his partner and their band, 'Awakening', and live on radio. They have also had a single released in the mid 90's.

Gary Markwick

www.palmistryinhand.com
www.reikiinhand.com
www.hypnotherapyholistic.com

Email g_markwick@hotmail.com

Contents

Now It Begins

Phase Three – Allowing, Accepting and Achieving

Phase Four – Being in the Present Moment

Now It Begins

Phase Five – Feeling Good about Yourself

Phase Six – Being Content

Phase Seven – Sixth Sense

Now It Begins

Now It Begins

The Great
Illusion

THE GREAT ILLUSION

My grandfather and mother were well known for their acts in the 1950's. They were called 'The Great Marlow and Georgina'. Their main act was mind reading which, of course, was an illusion. Like all great magicians, illusion is the key and like life itself, what we perceive mostly is an illusion, created by the way we think.

The things that we may take for granted, such as reading newspapers, magazines and watching television are great factors in fashioning how we live our lives. Every negative thing we see, hear and read about is unconsciously taken in and processed by our thoughts. As we think so we will be creating those things that we may not want in our lives. This, in turn, will affect everything, not only in ourselves, but in the world and the universe around us.

Since we were born, we have been told how to think, instead of trusting our own intuition and following our hearts. When we do not follow this, we may become anxious, stressed and possibly even ill, through worry. By serving the illusion, we are allowing ourselves to be drawn into all the complexities, distractions and the negativities that exist around us in this world.

The reality is the simplicity of life, the beauty which surrounds us, the appreciation for all things great and small. We do have the choice, and this choice is '*now*', when we come to understand, to know and accept the true reality. We then become open towards realising where our true purpose lies. Mainly because, when we learn the ways of this world we also lose so much. Through serving the illusion and not the reality, we will only eventually harm ourselves, becoming trapped and frustrated.

In this world around us, there is extreme wealth and extreme poverty, it is what we have created and allowed to happen, although it does not have to be this way. Some of us suffer with anxiety and depression, some of us become suppressed, and some of us become addicts.

Whichever way you look at it, we have allowed ourselves to be governed by other people, and we blame everyone else for everything that happens within our lives and the world around us, except for ourselves. This is the great illusion. It is now time to take responsibility for your life. We all have choice.

Buddha said: "through our desires comes suffering and human suffering is caused by ignorance."

So really, the key to all our desires and needs is balance. Without balance and discipline within our lives, we will eventually, destroy ourselves and humankind is destined to go this way unless we are willing to change. When we achieve balance within, we can change our lives for the better.

'The Secret Book of Knowledge'

There was once a young man who set off on his travels. One day, travelling through the desert somewhere in the East where nothing was to be seen for miles around, he came across a strange place, remote and hidden to the rest of the world. As he approached, it appeared to be a large building which looked like a fort or a palace. He could see the reflection of the sun in the beautiful stones embedded on the outside of the walls and the mosaic tiles surrounding them. The young man walked toward the fort, and as he came closer to the entrance, he noticed an old man on the turrets.

The old man was dressed in white, had a long white beard and wore a turban. He was looking down at the young traveller. Suddenly the large wooden and iron studded doors of the fort opened inwardly and the young man walked inside. He climbed the steps leading to the old man. As he stood before him, he saw he was holding a very large white book, embossed with gold leaf design. The young man was intrigued, and asked who he was.

The old man replied "I am the gatekeeper, I'm here to guard the secrets and I have been waiting for you a long time."

Now It Begins

The young man was taken aback. 'How could anyone possibly be waiting for me, especially for a very long time?' he thought.

"What does the large book that you hold so closely to you contain?" he asked the old man.

"This book holds all of life's secrets and great power, wisdom and knowledge. It is the answer to life itself and its meaning."

The young man became more and more interested, he tested the old man's veracity by asking questions to which he already knew the answers and to his amazement, the old man answered correctly every time. The young man was now desperate to know more and asked the old man if he could see what was inside this amazing book.

"Only those who are ready to see into the book of knowledge may look and you are not ready. For those who are ready to look there is no return and they must remain here to become its future guardian."

"I am ready," exclaimed the young man, his ego dominating. "What is it I need to do to be ready to look at the book?"

The old man said he would need to travel to seek and learn more discipline and wisdom, and then he may be ready. The young man had become obsessive with wanting to know what was in the book. What could it contain that could be so powerful as to know about all things in life?

The young man accepted the old man's instructions, and after spending the night he set off on his travels, always with the thought of eventually learning the secrets held in the book.

Months passed, and finally, he returned to find everything just as it was before. The young man approached the doors of the grand fort, as they opened he looked up to see the old man was standing in the same place. Once again, the young man stood before his elder, "Now I am ready to hold the book and look within."

The old man stared into the young man's eyes. Knowing the eyes are the windows of the soul and all can be seen through them, he said to the young man "No, you are still not ready. You must go to seek the knowledge within."

Once again, the young man, disappointed, set off reluctantly on his travels to experience many things and gain knowledge. He returned to the old man again only to be told he was still not ready.

As the years passed, the young man aged. He had almost forgotten about the amazing book which had once captured his heart. So he would occasionally remember and visit the old man only to be told the same as always. He was not ready.

The man who was once young himself had aged, and returned once again from his travels. The old man was dying. He stared into the young man's eyes and saw a great difference. "You are now finally ready to take my position and guard the book, if this is what you truly want."

The younger man was silent, deep in thought. After so many years of travelling and gaining so much experience of the world he had almost lost interest in the contents of the book.

Now, he was being put to the test, he had the choice to walk away, or to stay in the beautiful fort and its surroundings which were lost in time, and gain the knowledge that existed within this book. He finally came to a decision

"I have nothing else in mind to do. I have seen many things; I have travelled and have done most things anybody would wish to do. I have found love and lost love and now I am alone, yet, I am finally content with myself. So I have decided to stay, to take your place and the possession of the book and become the guardian."

The old man, passed him the book "It is yours" he said.

Now It Begins

Finally, after all these years, the great book had ended up in the palm of the younger man's hands. He slowly began to open the cover of the book. There was nothing on the first page. He turned the page, and still nothing. Turning the pages more quickly he discovered they were all blank. How could this be? He turned back through the pages furiously, with rage and disbelief. He could not understand why all the pages were empty sheets of paper bound within such a beautiful covering. He looked at the old man and said, "What is the meaning of this? They are all blank. There is absolutely nothing whatsoever inside of this book."

The older man turned to him; "You have travelled much, you have gained much wisdom. Therefore you should know all true knowledge and wisdom is gained through our experiences throughout life, and is contained, and comes from within. You have already mastered this, and now have no need to know what this book might hold. You already have the answers."

The old man laughed out loud. The younger man was very angry at first, and then suddenly, he saw the light. He realised, something which was so simple, yet, he had overlooked it for so many years. He also began to laugh out loud, and as he did something strange happened. Suddenly, the beautiful surroundings of the fort disappeared, he looked around and all was gone. When he turned back again towards the old man, he had also disappeared, and the book had became an old piece of wood and the once magnificent fort was no longer.

We all serve the illusion from time to time, but when we are able to see through it, we become open to reality. Then and only then can we understand and know our true selves and our purpose in life.

These are important and exciting times for us all to be living in, as we are now entering into a new phase in our lives, though not everyone will be aware of this. It is a shift raising our levels of vibration to a higher state of consciousness, becoming more in touch and aligned within ourselves. Where our minds and thoughts may cause confusion, our hearts will tell us the truth of what we need to know. The old world is now passing as we enter into a new one. This is all about letting go of the control we have been taught in the past. Taking control of our own lives takes us where we want to go or be. For those, who are wishing to change their lives for the better; we can bring all this towards us easily and effortlessly.

One of the main purposes for this change on earth is to awaken from the greed and selfishness that has governed the planet for a long time.

It is now time to work from your heart. The only way forward in this world is to connect with each other, to share and network, to change our ways, our thoughts and actions and give unconditional love in the hope that we may change the world we live in to a better place. Those who resist will create more difficult times ahead. For those who are aware and have awakened, will understand it is a necessary process, and the only way forward is by helping one another. It is now time to change and awaken, as we have been asleep for too long. Even those who once laughed at certain statements made about new age concepts, are now listening carefully. They may still not have come to terms with it, but are now taking an interest.

This reawakened energy which is uplifting to us all, is changing the world in which we live. It is a vibrational energy which is raising our awareness to a higher level of consciousness. I believe greater forces are now at work to show us the way forward, in these desperate times before we destroy ourselves. I say it is reawakening, as we have all been here before.

It is Now a Time to Remember.

The book of Revelations describes it perfectly. It says 'I will come as a thief in the night and take from you everything that you have, if you are unaware and asleep, and you will not know which hour I come.' We are being prepared for great changes to come as this is the time for cleansing, replenishing, and renewal, letting go of the past and of what no longer serves us anymore, as this is a new beginning, a new age with exciting times.

Now It Begins

In the past we have been conditioned and suppressed with limiting thoughts and beliefs. This has existed for thousands of years. We did not understand all things were possible. Often when we did, through certain philosophies, it was taken from us by others who sought to gain control, leaving us in a powerless and confused state of mind.

Astrologically, we are entering into the Age of Aquarius, which is supposedly, a time of freedom for humanity, creating balance and harmony. In the Hindu religion, the reign of the god Kali is now coming to an end, which also signifies the end of one cycle and the beginning of a new one. These times have also been prophesised for thousands of years by the ancient Central American civilisation the Mayans, predicting a shift and the end of a cycle in this period of time in which we are living now.

The Mayans were an advanced civilization and had also predicted long ago great changes to come in the world, which is all part of the vibrational shift that is happening today. The Mayans were very accurate with their astrological calculations and could count in hundreds of thousands.

It would seem that our western calendar has been based on the Mayan one, with two changes up to the present date, and these are the Julian and Gregorian Calendars.

The beginning of the Mayan calendar dates from 11 August, 3114 BC until December 21st, 2012 AD. The

Now ItBegins

Mayans have said that the merging of the dark and the light comes into force on the 21st Dec 2012 creating a greater awareness for all beings.

2012 was always the completion of the ancient Mayans long count calendar. This is known as the great cycle, creating new beginnings and bringing us into more harmonious times, the closing of one great cycle and the opening of another.

This is the beginning of a new world of transformation and change.

These changes have already begun and are gradually taking us to higher levels of understanding of ourselves and each other!

Given this collision of cycle changes, some think it is the end of the world as we know it. It is not the end; it is the beginning of this new shift which is happening within us.

We can also see many changes happening in the world around us, the climate, recession and other catastrophes. We have chosen to be here at this great awakening to help with the new vibrational time shift and many people are beginning to open up and, as I like to think; remember, as I believe we all know these things already. It is now our time to realise this universe was created for us and everything is here for

Now It Begins

us and the world to enjoy, moving on to new beginnings. A new world is emerging, a new awakening.

This book will show how to gain strength within these troubled times gaining practical and spiritual knowledge and awareness.

Trusting in the Flow of Life

All life exists within cycles and there are also many cycles within our lives (of which, I will speak about later on). These indicate changes. When it is time to move on we need to make the decision to change. Resisting these changes means not only will we miss opportunities we have waited for but we may bring heavier burdens and responsibilities upon ourselves which we do not want or no longer require. By not accepting changes within our lives, possibly through some unfinished business which may not have been dealt with, we are not letting go of the past, we are then not allowing ourselves to trust in the flow of life through our higher selves. The universal cosmic energy or spiritual force knows what we need and knows what is right for us. Trust in this and your life will flow, without the need of control. When we resist the changes of life, we become stuck in the past. Let go and stop holding on to those reigns of control.

As the world is changing fast, a great shift of universal energy is taking place. Some of us are

Now It Begins

aware of this and are ready to move forward and leave behind an old world that has suffered from greed, selfishness, anger, blame and hatred. This means, raising our vibration of energy from within and connecting with one another on a higher and faster frequency that is happening now on this planet. For some this is inconceivable and for others, the transformation has already begun.

It is like a portal that has opened up, allowing us to enter into a new dimension whilst here on earth. The gateway may not remain open for very long, it is giving us the choice to enter, but will eventually close. After this, it will re-create a greater division between people, although one with a universal balance of the lower and the higher true self, as all humans have their purpose to help one another.

For those who are open to receive the gift, they will become more in touch with other like-minded beings, and will have a greater purpose on this earth. This gift allows them to work with the higher self as well as with the earth, to assist those who may not be quite ready to move with the shift.

However, let it be remembered, that we are all connected to the one source and the most important part of this transformation is to go beyond the ego of our thoughts and open our hearts by having a greater understanding of one another with equality and unconditional love, as we are all beings of light.

We are all going through great changes in these

Now It Begins

uncertain times and it is now time to stop analysing the confusion that exists around us, especially on a material level, which is of a slower and denser frequency. This material level is our lower and primitive self. There are many who will continue to remain and work on the slower vibration of the lower self; each person has their purpose to contribute to the world so that it may change in whatever aspect that may be. Others will now realize that they need to fulfil something greater than ever before within their lives in a positive and altruistic way, to help the world before destruction may be inevitable, we have the choice.

When we open our hearts and let go of what no longer serves us and accept who we truly are, we then become free of restrictions that have held us back for so long. We do this by surrendering - the Universe, always knows best what our true needs are. We cannot take the whole world upon our shoulders no matter how strong we may be; it is now time to network and help one another.

Do not limit yourself to believing in only what you may see around you, this is the illusion, go beyond and see the reality. It is only fear that holds us back from being free. Those who have sought control over others in the past have indoctrinated that fear into us.

For those who say, "I do not believe," well, non-belief is a form of belief within itself and for those who are

Now It Begins

open to accepting the changes to come; a great spiritual awakening is now taking place. In reality, there is no separation between us.

It is now time to stop serving the illusion and see the reality

It is your
awakening.   **So,**

NOW IT BEGINS.

Phase One

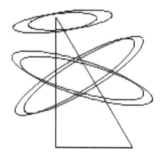

Changing Your Life

Phase one

Changing Your Life

Changing Your Life

Many of us are now searching for ways to ease the pressures in these stressful modern times, especially with economic and ecological decline. Wondering what will come next, as the world is changing so quickly. Entering this new shift is one reason for these changes. A higher vibrational energy is raising awareness of the planet and human consciousness. There will also be a greater division between people, as some will accept the changes and some will resist. There will be those who are working on a higher level of energy and those working on a lower level. Each one has their purpose. This chapter explains why some people will be feeling more unbalanced, uncertain and insecure; causing confusion and not knowing what may lie ahead for them in the future.

As we become more spiritually aware and advanced, many in this world will also become more aggressive with hatred, anger, jealously and with greed. This is the division, the yin and yang, and the balance. A new world is now emerging and taking shape as the old one is gradually fading. We can only go forwards, and the only time is 'Now!' The veil from our past has been lifted, and it is now time for action.

Now It Begins

Through knowing ourselves from within and who we truly are, we can change certain things about ourselves, which may have been bothering us throughout our lives. When we begin to know ourselves and not just the part of us that we have been conditioned to, from a set pattern that has been learned in our past, we can then know our soul purpose. This will give us guidance as to why we are here on this earth, and what purpose we may serve. Our true soul purpose for humankind is to serve one another. By doing this, we free ourselves from the restrictions and limitations we may have created for ourselves. This is the only way forward, by sharing and communicating with one another and working together on a higher level of vibration.

As for everything that happens in our lives, there is always a reason and a purpose. Nothing happens by chance.

You can change your life now by remembering who you are!

Accepting Yourself and Others

It all begins by starting to like yourself and accepting 'You' for who you really are. The more we can do this, the more positive attitude you will have about yourself. Whatever we have learned and understood in life is also what we are sending out to the world through our thoughts. This is what returns back to us,

Now It Begins

and is then anchored through our feelings from within. By liking and loving ourselves unconditionally, we are learning to trust our feelings from within and connect to the natural flow in life. We can only take on what we are ready for at the time of learning and no more, but, whatever it is that you are about to take on board in your life, is right for you at the time, and that time is the present, which is now.

The Mirror Reflection

Now ItBegins

For some of us, it is often so much easier to see what we dislike in others and not always notice the same things about ourselves. Know we are all mirror reflections of one another. Everything that exists is energy. Whatever we send out through our thoughts to the universe, returns, thoughts create matter and materialise. When we blame others for certain things that go wrong within our lives, we are actually, in effect, harming ourselves. The biggest issue here is we need to take responsibility for our own actions. This is the only way we may move on in this world, otherwise, we dwell permanently in the past. There is always something to learn, what may seem to be another person's fault, might well be of our own making.. We are all mirror images of each other. The likes and the dislikes we may see in others, is actually a reflection of ourselves and like attracts like, as we attract and create everything through our thoughts. The same principle applies to how we perceive life, whether we acknowledge it or not.

Next time you notice something about another person which you may dislike, ask yourself if there might be any similarities between them and you. If you do not know what it is about them that you do not like, notice what you are seeing or hearing. What are you feeling? Is it the way they look, their hair, or clothes? Could it even be their name, which may have brought something up from your past that you dislike about them? Or, perhaps you may notice something about the other person which makes you feel good. It may be a positive trait, or a negative one. Whatever it is, gain knowledge from this experience.

You must be careful what and how you think, as every thought will transform your life and the world in every way it possibly can, for better or for worse. This is the universal law. When we learn to use our intuition (and for those of you who do not know how, I will guide you later on in this book) and by tuning into your higher selves we can be guided not only to knowing ourselves, but to avoid certain mistakes which we or others may make before they even happen.

The key to all of this is acceptance. Accepting ourselves, and accepting what another person may be showing us at the time. We all have messages for each other. Look within for the communication and connection of what each message might offer you. By using our intuition and inner guidance, we can know a great deal more. Allow your thoughts to flow with your true feeling and work from your heart. Your heart will speak and tell you the truth; your head may cause confusion at times.

Why do things keep happening in our lives?

Mainly because of the way we think.

Now It Begins

Everything in life has a purpose with nothing happening by chance and from everything there is a lesson to be learned. When we have simply not learned the lesson we have been taught, then it will be repeated as many times as necessary until we have finally grasped it and we are then ready to move on. There will always be obstacles in life, but usually, when we have dealt with them, they will not be repeated.

It is said 'It is a long journey from the head to the heart.'

Whatever you are thinking about at any time, you are also attracting. It is important not only to think positive, but to remain in the present time. When we project our thoughts continuously into the future worrying about things that might happen we create negativity. Old habits, regrets and resistance to change make it difficult to stay in the present. When, through fear and doubt, we project our minds into the future we are constantly pursuing something, instead of allowing it to happen naturally, and bringing towards us what it is we really want in life. We end up driving these things away.

Look into the mirror for a few minutes every day. Stare at your own reflection and tell yourself you like what you see. Give yourself positive affirmations.

Now It Begins

For example:

I like and accept myself for who I am or I am a good and loving person.

Each and every day as I stare into the mirror my confidence grows as I now believe in myself.

The Presence of Now

This is why it is important to remain in the present time. Of course, everything has its purpose, and the past and the future have theirs. Do not get caught up in other people's energy, if you can help it. We often spend too much time wondering or worrying what others might be thinking. When we compare ourselves with others, we are losing and draining our own resources from being able to achieve the things we want. Through comparing, we can become envious, jealous and possibly bitter towards others, leaving us feeling low and a lack of self esteem, or even angry and aggressive. In this modern day society, we have access to all things, and we can now see, hear and know how others live their lives in the world around us. In one respect, this is very positive, because communication brings us closer together. In another way, for many, it can bring destruction. This has always been the way of the world. However, things are now progressing at a faster rate than ever before, creating great changes.

Now It Begins

*Happiness can only exist in the presence of
now. Be content and know yourself.*

Embracing Responsibility

This is a time to start taking responsibility for
ourselves and stop blaming others for what we are
lacking in our lives. We can only attract things in life
which we truly want when we are feeling good about
ourselves. When we feel unhappy, we are most likely
to attract negativity. If we continue to focus on
negativity, we will most surely create ill health and
bring the very things into our lives that we do not
want. Positive thoughts are the key to happiness. This
is one of the laws of the universe. It is the universe
saying to us 'Why should you be given what you
want, when you do not even appreciate what you
already have.'

It is so important for us to accept and appreciate all
we have, all we have been given, no matter how little,
before we can move on in life. After all we have
attracted everything that has come into our lives.
Before we come down into this present life, we
choose everything about ourselves, our parents, who
we are, and where we are going in life. We forget all
of this when we are here because if we always knew
the future, we may not always like what we see. It is
our purpose to remain in the present time and believe
we can, and are, achieving our soul purpose in life.
Many believe our true soul purpose is external. In a

way, this has some truth, but our real soul purpose in life is internal.

Everything has a purpose and nothing happens by chance, we all connect through vibrational energy and through the same source. As above, is below. The sky is a reflection of the sea; the heavens are reflections of the earth. We attract each other through the vibrations we send out. We bring people towards us in our life for a purpose in order to understand what it is we need to learn about ourselves. Some believe after our life has ended on this earth; we enter into an environment similar to the one with which we are familiar and have created on this earth, as is the same for our past lives. What we have made of our lives today is a result from our past. By using our intuition and inner guidance we can know all things.

To look within our Hearts is to look within our Soul, for this is where the soul is found.

Anger

There are times when we get upset by others, we get angry with the way they behave, or the way they act. We may feel frustrated and when the anger is turned inwards may even become depressed. These feelings can suppress us from being our true selves; they take away our internal power. It is time to listen to what our feelings are saying. The more we learn acceptance for ourselves and others, the greater our ability will be to understand. When we become angry with others, it is usually something to do with ourselves, something which we may not have seen coming. The person we are angry with may be showing us something about ourselves we have not yet seen. If we had seen this confrontation beforehand, it would not have happened. There will also be a lesson to be learned, this lesson will reappear from time to time, until we are ready to accept and let go of it. Those that love us the most give us the greatest lessons.

As above is below we are all reflections of one another and through this we learn to create balance and harmony within.

Letting go

Now It Begins

We may not be able to change the past, but we may certainly be able to change the way we feel about it. Holding onto negative thoughts and emotions may cause one to worry and become anxious, which may eventually lead to more serious issues in life as we build and store them in our unconscious minds. Those thoughts become trapped. By letting go of what no longer serves a purpose in our lives, we can begin to learn who we are, where we are going, and what we truly want and need in our lives. The focus is within. The more we are able to quieten our minds and relax, the easier it becomes to filter out the unnecessary information that builds up in our minds, constantly disturbs us and distracts our thought process. It hinders concentration, blocking what we are trying to achieve and create. Suppressing emotions over a period of time with no escape route can be likened to a pressure cooker which will eventually blow. The outcome could even lead to a nervous breakdown or other serious complications.

The Story of the Little Snail

There were three snails sitting on the side of a river bank. The river below was flowing fast and furiously, and would surely take anyone and anything with it once in its deep waters. As the snails remained firmly stuck tight to the muddy bank of the river, lazing around and passing the time of day, one of them had an inspirational thought. This inspired thought had come from no known place that the snail was ever aware of, but it was so intense, it occupied his thoughts completely. The intuitive thought he had received when lying quietly on the bank with nothing else to do was in fact to 'let go'. This also came as a great shock as; 'who in their right minds would do such a thing?', 'it would be plain suicide'. However, 'let go and be free!' was certainly the message he was hearing so clearly.

The message was becoming very intense and worrying. It seemed to the snail he had reached the time when he had to make a decision which would change his life forever. If he decided to stay where he was for the rest of his life, he would never forget the time of that intuitive awakening and would always wonder if he had made the right decision. He looked around at the scenery, the place where he had decided to live and then gazed upon the other two snails who had become his friends. Many questions raced through his mind; 'what will happen to me if I let go?', 'what if I die?', 'what about my friends?' Deep down he had already made up his mind because he had wanted to change his life for a long time. He used to wish for so many things, never believing they would ever come true.

We all have dreams. Often they may come to us when we least expect them. The snail calmed his mind, entering into a relaxed state. 'OK, I have made my decision, I am going to let go.' This is the only way to make the correct decision in our lives, in a calm and relaxed state.

Now It Begins

The snail said a final farewell to his friends and surroundings and gave his thanks and appreciation to all things.

He let go of the bank. It all happened so quickly. As he hit the water, he was swept away from the place he had once lived; he did not even have time to look back at the life he had led. This was a frightening experience for him. The current of the water was so fierce it began to take him under. It was not his intention to drown. He was confused as he continued to sink, going deeper and deeper into the vast depth of the water. As he was plunging to his death, he suddenly said; 'Oh well, I have made my decision, it was my choice, and no one else's, I have let go!' He had almost reached the bottom of the river. But quite a dramatic change had occurred because not only had he made a decision by letting go, but he had also made a decision to 'Accept'.

As soon as the snail accepted the consequences, a miraculous thing happened. The tiny snail began to rise and emerge to the surface of calmed waters. He was free! He had made his decision, he had let go, accepted and now he lives a very happy life with old and new friends alike!

When we are able to free ourselves from the restrictions of our past, we are open to receiving all things that are possible. When we connect with the universe we create the power within.

Now It Begins

Here is a key towards transforming and changing our lives for the better.

The first stage: *Our dreams and desires.*

The second stage: *Using the power of intentions.*

The third stage: *Letting go.*

The final stage: *Acceptance.*

Wherever you may travel to in life, and whatever it is you may do, if you are not flexible about the way you perceive things, eventually, there, will become here, and here will become there. In other words, all things in life that you may do will just be a repetitious cycle from your past. It becomes important to know what it is you really want. Often there is no turning back, as the grass is not always greener on the other side. Your desires must come from not only being in the present state, but from **being** happy within, and not from a state of fear. If we focus on a negative state of mind this anchors greater anxiety.

However, whatever decision you may make, is the right one for you at the time.

Intentions

If we can focus our intentions on working for the good of the planet, the human race, and if our intentions are pure towards helping others, then surely and truly will it return and magnify. The energy is one. Good intention is power.

Now It Begins

It is important to focus on our intentions and goals at all times and not be diverted by any negative outside influences.

After we have decided what our good intentions are, detachment is important and necessary. With detachment we can achieve and bring all things towards us effortlessly. The belief is within us. When we become too attached to certain things in life we may choose goals which can create negativity through our insecurities in being obsessed with them.

By 'detachment' I mean giving ourselves permission to let go of those things in our lives, either mental or physical which hinder us from moving towards achieving our intentions.

With detachment we free ourselves, trust and accept we have planted the seed and now allow it to grow into something as strong as an oak tree.

The groundwork has now been done. **It is time to let go. Surrender. Detach and trust the universe is working for you.**

There will always be obstacles in our lives this is a necessary process so we may learn and understand from them. Where there is unfinished business it is much easier to deal with it when detaching, returning to it later when we are recharged, refreshed and our energy is stronger. It is akin to allowing ourselves to

Now It Begins

feel good after a nice relaxing break.

Even if the universe does not give us what we want at the time, it will definitely give us what we need most and for this we should be thankful every day.

Be open to whatever may come your way as this can be a blessing in disguise.

Why is it so hard to let go?

We become so attached in life to the things which serve us best at the time, but, when they may no longer serve a real purpose anymore, or, when it is time for us to move on in life, we tend to hold on and remain attached to some things from our past.

It may still be serving a purpose by not letting go, because everything has a positive by-product. Just like the person who would like to stop smoking, but cannot. Possibly their need to smoke at the time, may be greater than the need to give it up. Our imagination is much stronger than our willpower. For example; as soon as someone has a thought of quitting smoking or losing weight, their imagination may well conjure up an image of the calm feeling they associate with smoking a cigarette or how comforting it is to eat a bar of chocolate. The imagination wins every time. It is through our unconscious mind, our higher self, we create all things using our imagination. When we use our imagination and thoughts in a positive way, however; seeing and imagining yourself

Now It Begins

becoming healthier and slimmer than you ever were before, then, and only then, will this happen. Utilising our imagination and visualising in this way, we can achieve and bring all those things we want toward us. It is a powerful tool when used in the correct way. It can destroy our future progress when used in a negative way. The mind will take care of the body. Every thought will eventually shape and change the way we see, hear, feel, smell and taste.

With every thought, we become who we are, and with this, we can help to change the world for the better. Changes are inevitable; our world has recycled many times in the past. Even the bible says Adam and Eve were here to replenish, to renew and start again.

So, next time, when changes are occurring in your life, take notice of what they are. Get in touch with your inner feelings, your higher self, and ask within what it might be telling you. Remember, everything has a purpose, and the smallest messages we receive when we are in tune with ourselves may be the greatest. Do not be afraid of change. It is a natural part of our progression. It is the path which leads us to our true destiny. When we restrict or block this path, we restrict ourselves; we block growth because we are not allowing ourselves to receive what we truly deserve. Be non-resistant and float like water. By letting go and surrendering we overcome resistance we allow ourselves to take the journey into the unknown, where all things can be achieved and created.

Now It Begins

I am now letting go of what no longer serves me.
Whatever happens is all that will happen.
I surrender myself to the universe.
I will now enjoy myself by being and remaining in this present time.

Phase Two

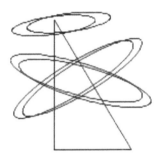

Changing the Way You Think

Phase Two

Changing the Way You Think

Changing the Way You Think

Do not be afraid of change!

Changing the way you think is the first principle of how the Laws of the Universe work. Your first thoughts are important, as this will shape the rest of your day and possibly the rest of your life. It would be best, if you can avoid focusing on the TV, radio, or newspapers, at least early in the morning or last thing at night. This is when we are most sensitive and possibly vulnerable to outside suggestions which may have a negative effect on our lives. When we watch the news on TV or read newspapers, we are attracting and exacerbating negativity. Even though you may not realise it, you have already started your day with negative thoughts.

Be aware of your everyday thoughts, what you are hearing, and what you are repeating to yourself. Also, be aware of what you are saying to others, and the words that you use. These can have great repercussions on our lives and others, and may create a domino effect. Negative thoughts are disseminated far more quickly than positive.

Now It Begins

How you think about yourself and others is shaping you and the world in which we live.

To change the way you think, be aware we do attract every thought that goes out in our lives.

This is our karma. It is the law of cause and effect.

Being Grateful

A good way to start the day, as soon as you awake, would be to give thanks, for being alive and for everything, no matter how small, which is meaningful to you in your life.

There are Buddhists monks in some countries who will wake in the early hours of the morning, chant and give thanks for surviving another day. Their appreciation is so great and yet their needs are so small.

It may become difficult to change your life unless you are grateful for what you have now. Once we respect what it is we do have and see it for what it truly is then we are ready to receive the things we truly deserve.

So as soon as you wake up you could say:

'I am so happy and very grateful for all good things in

Now It Begins

my life which come to me easily and effortlessly.'

'I am so happy and grateful for all the people who come into my life today and for all the lessons I have to learn from them.'

Removing Blockages

Negative thoughts can damage your health.

A build up of negative energy will not give you the dreams which you desire... Change your thoughts and be positive, clear negativity.

We need to learn to be non-judgemental. When we judge other people or, even ourselves by criticising and analysing, we are then creating a greater conflict within ourselves and placing too much thought on others. Rather than concentrating and focusing on our own abilities, reflecting who we really are and what we can achieve.

When we judge, we weaken those abilities within ourselves to achieve our goals. When we are feeling down or depressed, we cut off the flow of energy and create a blockage towards receiving the things that we deserve because, we are vibrating on a lower frequency than we would be if we were feeling good about ourselves. Give more time and more thought towards working on yourself. Remember positivity creates positivity. So, next time you find yourself

Now It Begins

being judgemental or criticising others, change this thought around from a negative to a positive and think, or say something nice about whatever it is you are judging or being critical of. Or, when someone or something is annoying you, try to see the situation in a different light. Turn it around and see a funny side to it. I know this can sometimes be hard for us all to do, but the more you practise this, the easier it will be become.

This can also be the same when we blame others for things which go wrong in our lives. It is now time to take responsibility for ourselves and our actions.

Whenever you catch yourself thinking negative thoughts try to bring yourself back into a good frame of mind.

If there is a time, when you are feeling down, smile. When you smile it becomes almost impossible to feel down. Feel good about yourself.

If you are feeling low, detach yourself from whatever it is that you are doing. Go for a walk preferably somewhere you can be around nature.

Nature has tremendous energy. Trees, for example, have been around for a long time, and are great reservoirs for giving and receiving energy. Native American Indians have always respected trees as much as the earth, and called them the 'standing people'. Walk, breathe deeply and appreciate your surroundings. This is the start of bringing the good things back into your life. The more you practise changing your mindset, with positive thoughts, the easier it becomes to send negative thought patterns away, removing the blockages and changing your life for the better.

Changing the Past

The more we become aware of our natural state of being, our conscious and unconscious minds and using our intuition, the more we will learn to create a balance and learn to heal ourselves from within. We have all the resources we need. If we can learn to look from within, we can know outwardly the answers for our future and where our destiny lies. OK, we may not necessarily be able to change the past, because it has already happened, but, we can most certainly change the way we think and feel about it in the present.

One way to change your feelings about the past is to use visualisation and see the situation in your mind's eye.

Here is an exercise for changing the way we feel about the past:

First, allow yourself to relax. Using visualisation, see in your mind's eye a negative scene which created a

Now It Begins

problem in your past. Do this more than once, until you become familiar with this process.

When this becomes clear in your mind allow the negative image to fade and come back into the present time.

Now visualise beautiful scenery or somewhere you may have been, like a favourite place, somewhere you have really enjoyed yourself in the past. See yourself relaxing in this favourite place. When you have achieved this state, having totally detached from the negative one, think how you would like to change the original negative scene into a positive one.

Once you have done this see yourself in a positive state of mind and wellbeing in the picture. If you cannot see yourself in the visual image, then just feel it.

When the positive image has been installed, allow this process to work from your thoughts and through to your feelings. The end result must be felt!

After this exercise ground yourself by taking some deep breaths and imagine your feet feel as if they are sinking into the ground, and you are becoming stronger with every breath you take. Afterwards, give yourself positive affirmations. 'Feeling good and positive about yourself, every day in every way my life is getting better and better'. Practise this whole

Now It Begins

procedure several times until you really feel it is working for you, changing your life for the better. Remember, you are changing your feelings about a negative situation which happened in the past into a positive one.

This kind of positive imagery can work through issues of the past, our present and our future.

Of course, this exercise for changing the way we feel about our past, does not necessarily solve the problem at the time. For this, it must be recognised and dealt with as soon as possible, so we do not repeat the same mistakes again. Although by becoming more aware and changing the way we think and feel about a situation from our past, we can prevent certain things from happening and change our outlook in the present and for the future.

The mistakes we make in life are often repeated until we have learned the lessons they are teaching us. When we have learned these lessons, there will no longer be any need to repeat them. It is only unfinished business which returns.

Giving from our hearts is fine, and a wonderful thing to do, as long as we know where our boundaries may lie, and also by letting others know and respect them too. We all have our limits to what we can give to others. When we give too much of ourselves, it may leave us feeling drained of energy, and could even engender regrets and resentment. There will always be someone, or even many who will be present to take advantage of generosity.

Never stop giving, as this is the greatest gift, and for those who are givers in this world, they are truly blessed. Just know where your balance lies.

Self Power

We must work on changing ourselves. As one's thoughts expand, it will have a positive effect on others, creating a greater awareness. When a person has a positive thought, many people will pick up their energy and vibrations, as this person, is sending energy out in wave form. The same, of course, will work on the negative vibration; this is another reason why we need to train our minds to have positive thoughts, remember like attracts like.

In the past, you may have noticed when you have been around or talking to a person, after you have left them you are suddenly feeling totally drained of energy. The person, who has left you feeling this way, is possibly working and vibrating on a lower energy. Sometimes, this is done deliberately, by the other person as some are like emotional vampires and enjoys stealing people's energy.

Others may not even know they are sending out this kind of energy, as they are victims of circumstances, needing help and attaching themselves to others for support by being the poor me. We all need to give and receive from time to time. We all need help and to give help, but we also need to say no to others.

When we deny our self power, others will take it from us.

The power from within is not something we need to control or for which we need to fight. This kind of power is external, using force. The true self power comes from within. It is going beyond the ego, and being humble to yourself and others, and most of all, it is about knowing yourself and who you are. Those who try to control others in their lives will not succeed for long, as we all have free will and choice. Those who use this control are coming from a position of ignorance, jealously or greed. This kind of power usually comes from their past. There can be many reasons for this behavioural pattern.

I have visited many countries in which superstition and black magic seems to rule people's lives in one way or the other. In the western world this has faded over time, but it is still prevalent in other parts of the world. Individuals and whole villages live in fear of curses and spells which may have been cast upon them from others. Many believe they have been cursed and for this reason nothing is, or will go right in their lives for them, or so they have been told. I have met many people who have become victims of such beliefs. I have been asked many times if I can

Now It Begins

remove spells from clients, and create ones to harm others, when I am working in London with palmistry. When they tell me they have been cursed, I tell them it is quite possible this has happened to you because you believe it to be true.

All things are possible through belief. When we believe others can be so powerful that they can take away from us what is rightfully ours - then it will happen. We surrender our powers, and give them to others who wish to control.

In the west, as well as in the rest of the world, this is often done in different ways. Those who manage to gain control over others are using their power externally by thought and often by sheer force and bullying. External power is not the same as using our self power internally. When we are using our powers externally and harming others it will always return to us. Those who try to control in this way, often prey on those who they think might be weaker than them, or more sensitive. Quite often, the one who is on the receiving end becomes the victim leaving them feeling drained of energy or confused, and giving away something they may not have wanted to give.

This kind of power is external and thrives on fear. The person who controls lives with this fear does not know any other way, and will use this fear to manipulate others, to make them feel guilty, erode self esteem and create confusion and sadness in their lives.

Now It Begins

Of course, this is the law of the jungle and survival, everyone for themselves, and this was fine and necessary in the past, but now, we are moving on from those old fashioned ways and primitive times. We all have choice - and trying to control is not the way forward.

Our True Power comes from Within.

The eternal self power which lies within our soul and comes from the heart has no desire to do this. Once we have truly found it, we can know and have all the things we need. This is gained through the quietening of the mind, stillness, meditation, contentment and unconditional love. When we become in tune within ourselves, we can know all things which exist from the past, the present and the future.

We are all from the same source whichever way you describe it – the universe, the cosmos, god – an entire energy exists.

An entire energy exists and within the energy, there is no separation, regardless of our beliefs.

We are all one. We have come here to learn as spiritual beings gaining the experiences of being human. It is therefore, our soul purpose to help one another and to change this world from being so primitive in many ways, to one in which we would choose to live in harmony!

Now It Begins

Fears, Worries and Anxieties

Unconsciously, they may resurface from time to time, raising the fears, worries and anxieties which have been instilled in us from our past

This is why many people have trouble sleeping, and may wake throughout the night frequently or early hours of the morning, often, with cold sweats or palpitations.

There is nothing you can do by worrying about whatever it is that is bothering you. Remain in the present time, and know you will deal with it confidently and assertively if it comes.

Now It Begins

A client once came to me for hypnotherapy. After the session was over, I gave some techniques and exercises for helping them to overcome certain problems. One of these was showing the client how to remain in the present time. I asked them to repeat an affirmation, which is used in Reiki, 'just for today I will not worry', as many times as possible throughout the day. Before accepting this, the client told me that they had two children, and many other things, to worry about.

One of the symptoms this person was displaying was anxiety. I told the client they could do no more by worrying about a situation but, the more they remained focused on being in the present time, the stronger they would become within and would be able to deal with certain situations if and when they arose.

The key here in reducing our fears is being with people who have a positive outlook in life. Change your friends if they are dragging you down.

I have mentioned to friends I no longer read newspapers and seldom watch the news on TV. I have said I use my awareness to glean what I need to know in this world, and it has always presented itself to me, showing and giving me the answers I needed to know at that time, in one form or another. One of the friends replied 'There is no point in being oblivious and not know what is going on in this world!' I did not reply, and understood they were not ready for the statement I had made. Perhaps one day? Receiving certain information is essential to know what is happening in this world, but we also need to look within, and find a balance in our lives to understand what is true.

When you learn to let go and see the reality, you can move beyond the fears which hold you back!

Practise by staying and focusing in the present time!

You can do this by sitting in a quiet spot and letting your thoughts just pass by, as you relax. When one is not used to this procedure, many thoughts will surface, and may cause the person to be confused and anxious for a while. At this point, some will give up. Persevere.

In the same way, as when going for alternative therapies such as healing, the toxins are released in the body and rise to the surface, cleansing and clearing the blockages, making way for a new path of health. When this happens, sometimes the next day, or a few days after, a person who is not used to receiving this kind of treatment and one who may have deep rooted emotional issues, or, someone who has a great deal of toxicity in their body may feel a little unbalanced or unwell for a short time. Quite often the person may blame the healing technique or the healer for causing them to feel this way. However, more often than not, it is only the healing doing its work. When we accept this and recognise it for what it is, then, we can be cleansed, healed and are able to let go of issues which have been suppressing us for many years. Releasing the toxins and freeing ourselves, from guilt, jealousy, possessiveness, intimidation, feeling unloved and many emotions that have entrapped us in the past and have caused us to become slaves, victims, prisoners within ourselves.

'Now', is the only time to free ourselves as no one else can do this for you, others can help, but at the end of the day, it is up to you. You can show a person the way, but you cannot change them. This can only happen by you allowing it to happen; we have all suffered in one way or another at some stage in our lives. Admittedly, some more than others but, everything that happens, happens for a reason. If we can learn from those experiences we have had and use them to our advantage for the future, then we can achieve all things possible, and no longer remain a victim.

For every Loss there is an Opportunity

Many times in the past, I have lost certain things and opportunities after working hard building them up. The risks involved and the timing may not have been right. Or, it is possible I unconsciously expected to lose whatever it was I was holding on to, maybe through fear of what may happen in the future and

Now It Begins

also thinking and believing I did not deserve things like success and fame.

When I was young, and up to the recent past, whenever I had tried to do anything, my mother would always say to me I would not be any good at it. She would say; 'it would be too difficult' or; 'You have to be really good to do such a thing'.

This of course, would take away anyone's self esteem and confidence, especially as a child. As a result, at certain times in my life, when I bought a property (in fact we lost two in two recessions, and a business) or tried to get someone interested in my music (and I could go on), something would happen and they were lost.

Even though I usually get over things very quickly, it is always quite a shock when something dramatic happens.

These days, if something should happen in a dramatic and negative way, I like to think, 'That's interesting. Where is this leading to?' I wonder what will happen next, to create an equal amount of balance in a positive way, as there is always a balance. I will now, always look at a situation and the reasons why I may have attracted it in the first place. Of course, for every action there is a reaction and it was more than likely, I needed to learn a greater lesson each time, to bring me to where I am now at this stage in my life.

Now It Begins

For every loss, a new door can open with golden opportunities.

I have known many people to give up; some have even committed suicide. This is now happening so much in these times of desperation and confusion. They were pushed to the edge, just when help was around the corner. Never give up or lose faith. Miracles do happen, but not always in the way in which you think they will. I personally believe there is no escape from the things which we have not dealt with. So, just as we repeat the issues in this life, until we have learnt whatever it is we need to, it will be the same in the next one. As everything is a cycle!

Just like the story of the young man in the secret book of knowledge. It took me many years to realise finding myself and my true soul purpose was within me all the time, even though I felt I had one from an early age. You may travel the world several times over, and gain knowledge. Yet, you may never really find and know your true self. When we look within, we can know all things by just being in a confined space and detaching ourselves.

We do not always need to explore a great deal before we can find our inner peace. The path we have chosen can be a long and winding road for most of us, and the Karma which we accumulate from our past will be necessary to pay back. The challenges we also give ourselves, possibly before even coming down

Now It Begins

here on this earth, can be great. Whatever it is we need to learn before we are ready to move on and find balance, harmony and inner peace with ourselves can be a long journey. Though, we all have choice through our awareness, and it is now time we make this choice.

As I said before, I had always felt I knew my true purpose from as young as the age of three in a strange kind of way, yet, I still searched for many years. The feelings I had, were always the same throughout my life.

The experience of travelling the world and when helping others, it always came back to the same feeling, a sense of achievement in feeling good about myself and of what made me happy. Of course, at the age of three I was not aware of the experiences that I was to have in later life. What it was showing me, was an incarnation, a continual journey possibly, from a past life. I was aware of something that had already existed. This I knew, from a very early age. Like most of us, I had just forgotten. Everything is connected, and we are all connected and attached to something, but the things which can give us the greatest of pleasures in life are those of a simple nature, and we attract those pleasures from being detached, detaching ourselves from expectations of what might happen or, what may not. Again, it is trusting in the universe to show us the way without the need for control.

Now It Begins

Accept and allow it to happen, whatever happens.

Detachment

Detachment can also be, when allowing ourselves to step away from whatever it is we may want, or are trying to achieve in our lives at the time. When we become attached to something permanently in our lives, we are not seeing the bigger picture. We are not allowing the universe to do its work. In this way, it may lead us towards feeling insecure and even doubting everything is working for our good. With detachment we can free ourselves.

Ask. Surrender. Detach. Let go. This is where belief and true faith are everything; they are omnipresent and will stand the true test of time.

Remember though; to be thankful for what you have now.

Detach yourself from the outcome, instead of constantly checking to see if your wishes are being granted.

Let go, surrender, detach and trust the universe is working for you!

This does not mean you have to give up your wishes and desires.

Now It Begins

Plant the seeds, maintain and just let them grow!

Feel good and allow the confidence to grow from within as you are unique and there is no other you. Now smile and know that all good things are coming to you easily and effortlessly.

Phase Three

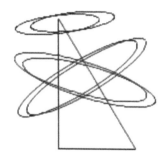

Allowing, Accepting and Achieving

Phase Three

Allowing, Accepting and Achieving

Allowing, Accepting and Achieving

By allowing the universe to create our goals, we are accepting changes and trusting in the flow of life. We are also accepting changes to take place within ourselves, allowing endless possibilities to be created. Trust in this and your life will flow, without the need to control. When we accept ourselves for who we are, we are allowing ourselves to receive what we truly do deserve. Do not be afraid of change, believe, allow and accept you deserve it.

It is so important to remain in this present time. 'The only time is now'. If we want to be happy, then we need to remain in the present. We can only change the future of the things we want by accepting ourselves for who we are in this moment in time.

When we accept the 'now', we can change the future. Otherwise our struggle with the present will create a future for things which we do not want. Acceptance of our self and our surroundings is the key to universal balance.

All these things we desire can only be created in this present time for the past has gone, and the future has not happened yet. The only time that exists is the present. Therefore, instead of trying to achieve our goals we create the possibilities by bringing it towards us into the now, and believing this is already happening, or that we have already achieved it.

We can only change the future of the things we want, by accepting ourselves for who we are in this moment in time. When we accept the now we 'CAN' change the future, otherwise we struggle with the present and create a future for the things we do not want. Acceptance of ourselves and our surroundings is the key to universal balance, when you are happy with yourself in the present you are creating happiness for your future.

We can achieve all things by acknowledging what it is we desire and then trusting in the power and wisdom of the universe, its energy and flow, to take care of it, by releasing our control over all things that we desire. When we do this, we surrender, we let go. Once this happens, it has a powerful and very effective way of working its way back to us, because we have freed ourselves of any burdens, worries and attachments which may have held us back from our past. The universal flow starts to work its magic within our lives.

When our minds are filled with worry about trying to achieve our goals, not only do we block off our own energy with negative thoughts but we stop ourselves from creating what we truly want and seeing who we

Now It Begins

really are, as there is no room to allow and accept the universal flow and energy!

All things can be created and achieved through non entity! We can bring all things towards us without having to struggle, we make our own limitations.

These are all powerful statements and work with the universe. Whatever you are focusing on, you will attract positive or negative.

When we have doubts, about how the laws of the universe work, we block off the energy which flows between us and the universe. It is so important, to believe this can and does work in our lives. The slightest amount of doubt will cancel the effects of what we are trying to achieve.

I use the word 'trying"; however, this is not the actual word to use when we want to attract or let go of something in our lives.

When we 'try', we can unconsciously, be trying too hard, forcing something and chasing away whatever it is we want to achieve. This might be because; we are actually projecting our will power into the future and possibly, trying to achieve something that not only, we may have doubts about achieving, but also, because we are not focusing on the present moment. It is so much easier to attract the things we want, by being and remaining in the present time, without the need for force or struggle. In this way, we bring

Now It Begins

towards us, whatever it is we want in this moment, and not chasing it away with doubts or moving into the future before we have it. Similarly, as discussed previously, it is easier to let go of things with this mindset.

Giving and Receiving

When we bring what we want into the present and believe we already have it, then we are attracting and manifesting our dreams.

If you can imagine; a gigantic Ferris wheel which turns in mid air. The wheel takes a very long time to complete a whole circle, sometimes many years, as it is different for whoever may stand before it. On the wheel, there are many platforms, and each platform is filled with all the things we could wish for in life. As we wait, for the gigantic wheel to go round, one of the platforms descends from above and comes down and stops in front of us. We notice all the beautiful things that are on the platform and then step on to it but, we take only what we need from it. When the next platform comes at a later date, we let go of what we have received from the previous time or, times before, providing it no longer serves a purpose any more, and then again, we take what is needed in the present time. We may not know beforehand when it is time to let go of whatever it is we need to let go of, but as we begin to know ourselves, we will know more of the things we need and what no longer serves us anymore. There can be a great difference between the things we want and the things we need.

Allow the energy to embrace you and feel the unconditional love which grows through you and around you. Let it spread. Receive it, and return it. As whatever we receive in life must eventually be returned at some stage.

In this life we only borrow. As we give, so shall we receive!

When we take too much in life, we create the suffering which affects others. Yes, we can bring and attract all things into our lives that we may wish for, but at the same time, we also need to create a balance. As we receive, we should also give. By doing this, we will create balance, and also create a feeling of well being, feeling good about ourselves for giving. We can have and attract the things we want in life, this is how the universe works, but there is also a need for balance when receiving equal to giving.

By giving from our hearts, we receive in every way, so have this thought in mind wherever you may go, or whoever it is you meet, the thought of giving and sharing with others is the key to great abundance. It is also about the understanding of how to receive, this will create harmony and balance within our lives, as being open to receiving is the same as giving. Many of us do not know how to receive. When someone gives us a gift and we accept it, it has the same energy as when we are giving out to others, which in return brings happiness. Giving can be in any form.

A thought given out every day to others and to the world can have a great effect.

There is Always a Price to Pay for Everything.

One of the main reasons why so many people are still starving in the world is because; we have in the past, and are continuing at even greater lengths, to take too much. We are also destroying everything around us.

Now It Begins

Wherever I have travelled in the world, passing beautiful scenery in the countryside as well as in the cities, people have trashed their surroundings. In India, the cows and pigs eat the waste and the remains of food that people have left, I have seen them eat paper and cardboard amongst other things, this has been the way for a long time, but the one thing any animal or human cannot digest, is plastic! This seems to be a problem which is increasing and is becoming out of control. I have seen this pile up, as well as other rubbish on the beaches, in the countryside and in the city streets, with plastic bags and plastic bottles left behind hotels. Possibly, it may be they cannot afford the machines to re-cycle. However, many of those beautiful places which once were like paradise on earth now have partly become rubbish dumps.

We are finding so many ways to destroy what was once so beautiful on this earth, we cannot go backwards to how things were, but, we can change our ways and preserve what we already have.

Many years ago, I was travelling across Borneo in Malaysia, and had heard about the deforestation there. I drove one day for seven or eight hours across the countryside searching for this deforestation. All I could see were small palm trees across the landscape for miles and miles in the distance. The penny dropped. The rainforest had already been chopped down and replaced with these new trees which had been planted for their oil, because they grew very fast

Now It Begins

and would bring in great wealth. Where did all the animals disappear to? We are creating catastrophes. This was one of the original primate rainforests on earth, just like the Amazon, dating back thousands of years from when it all began and it had been destroyed.

Whatever we are taking out of this world will need replenishing at some point. Otherwise, it will all cease to exist. This may happen in a natural way eventually and nature does have its own way of taking care of things and creating a balance. However, while we are here, it is our duty also to take care of what we have now, and to teach this to the generations of the future.

Learn from old cultures, like the Shamans who learned to respect the earth by taking only what is needed and not for the want of desire and greed. The children of certain native tribes were taught to go and take from the trees and pick only the fruit which would be given to them. The children might have said; 'How will we know what is given to us'? The elders would reply; 'You will know' meaning taking only the fruit which has fallen to the ground. This may seem only symbolic to some but we can all learn from this by using our awareness to its full potential whenever we are able.

Many cultures from our past have made offerings to what, or whoever they have believed in. It is showing their appreciation towards giving something back in return for what they have received. This, in itself, is

Now It Begins

creating a balance. We are all here to serve one another and it is now time to show respect. Give to all things, no matter how small or great they may be and respect them, it will return. You may possibly think we may not always be able to change some things, because at the time, they are beyond our control and we cannot do everything. No, you cannot, but by doing something in the way you know, we will most certainly make significant changes for our future and for the better.

All living creatures on this earth serve their purpose in one way or another. No one is any greater or lesser than the other, even though we are sometimes led to believe this!

We are entering into a new world; a world in which we can create a balance for ourselves, others and our planet. It can be your heaven or your hell. We all have choice and as we all know, it has reached the point where it is a race against time.

Lyrics taken from one of my songs

One last Dance

Unless we all sit down and try
To make things better now
Given any reason to deny
And the whole world tumbles down
Cause it's the last dance

Now It Begins

The 'Giving Away' Ceremony

Before the last century, the Native American Indians from different tribes would all come together once a year for a ceremony. Each tribe would choose an item of great value. These would be personal treasures that they owned and may have been passed down from their ancestors. Tribes from all over came and met at a certain place. Many of them would be enemies of the other tribes which were there. Yet, on this special occasion, all hostilities were left behind and they would honour each other by giving these personal treasures to one another. Once they had offered and exchanged gifts, these were then accepted and totally respected; it would have been a disgrace for them not to have been.

After the turn of the last century, the American government banned this ceremony (as well as others) because they felt all the tribes were humiliating themselves and were making themselves poorer with the giving away ceremony (or this was the excuse they made). This ceremony was all about respect and appreciation, even if it had only lasted for a short period of time. What could have been a greater way of giving, giving to their enemies, or of their most cherished possessions which may have been in their family for centuries? This is giving truly from the heart as these people who had so little and had great pride, gave something which was so precious and so meaningful.

Now It Begins

Sometimes an offering or making a sacrifice of some kind is often necessary to reconcile, to show our forgiveness or appreciation and to free ourselves from our past and show our respect. Giving is not about what one should have to do, if you feel this way, then, it is better not to give at all. I have seen many people around the world very confused about what they should or should not give to beggars or to the local people who are in need. I always say to them; 'Give from your heart and do not question it in your head' When you have to think about what you are going to give or what you have already given, not only will it create more confusion but the good deed will be cancelled out.

Admittedly, there are so many scams around. One guy, who had prosthetics, artificial legs, was on the local beach in India near where I stay and was asking for money. Later on in the same day, and on more than one occasion, some tourists had seen him remove his legs and run into the sea! Scams like these, have and always will exist, but it does not mean we have to stop giving. Use your intuition and know what is true. If it feels right; do it. Whatever you give let it be meaningful to you! Here is a statement in the bible which says: 'When giving to others, do not let your left hand know what your right hand is doing'. Another one says: 'Do not blow your trumpet when giving'.

There is a piece from a book called; 'The way of the Sufi' by Idries Shah. It is about a poor, humble but enlightened man who lived in the middle ages who is a Sufi (Sufism is a Middle Eastern spiritual philosophy). The poor man is invited by a very wealthy man to his house, who owns all the land around him and the majority of the property in the town.

The wealthy man has invited the poor man, to see his collection of jewels. The poor man enters the house and views the beautiful collection of jewels, he then, thanks the wealthy man for showing it to him and says 'Thank you for showing your collection of jewels to me, they are very beautiful, although, in many ways, I am a much wealthier person than you.' The rich man said 'How can this be? I have everything which anyone could possibly want.' The poor man replied 'I now walk away as a free man, where as you must guard your treasures, like being in prison.'

Think what it is that you really want in life before making any quick decisions. Everything has its price. As John Lennon of the Beatles once said; 'Be careful what you wish for, it might come true'.

To be content in life is the ultimate, which I will discuss further in Phase Six. It is everything we may strive for but, quite often, we miss the point because contentment can only exist in the present time. When we are totally content within, we have all we need, and have no need to want and chase the things we may not necessarily need in our lives anymore. We can all have and take too much. If you give a child too much, you will stifle them and he or she will never appreciate what has been given.

I always wondered for many years when travelling to countries which had a lot of poverty, why the children and many adults appeared to be happy and were always laughing and smiling despite, how poor they were. Many children have even given gifts to me or my partner, even though we were total strangers to them.

Now I believe, I know the answer, even though I am still learning and understanding countries like India after many years. In these countries there is still respect, the children have not quite caught up with the western world, although this is changing fast through world communications.

One does not need wealth for contentment or happiness, as true happiness lies within. Those who have less will often give more than those who have more. This can in many ways create happiness and contentment. I am not talking about what one can give in the material sense or judging the status of a person. This in truth has little value and it is the illusion we have created through giving to suit ourselves, in which we might expect praise. As I mentioned before, what really counts is giving from the heart. It is far greater for a person to reach into their wallet or purse and find they have very little left, only enough to see them through to the next time money may come and yet, still give something of what little they have left. This is giving from the heart; it has true value and holds the greatest rewards.

To know true happiness and contentment is to know ones self, it does not rely or feed on desires or greed, power and corruption. In fact it is the opposite; it is humbleness, honesty, generosity and being in the present.

Why is it that many people who have so little can give so much?

The Little Old Blind Lady who Gave so Much

When I was in my late teens to very early twenties, one of the jobs I had was working for a company called Victoria Wines. I used to deliver the wines and soft drinks to very large houses in a wealthy part of North London. One road was known as Millionaires' Road. I also delivered to other houses, in a not so wealthy part, not far from there. Within this area; one of my customers was a little old lady who lived on the ground floor of a council estate. Every week on a Friday afternoon, I would deliver to her door two small bottles of Guinness and one small bottle of stout.

The little old lady would be very polite and invite me inside of her apartment. She asked me to place the beers on the table where the money would be waiting

Now It Begins

for me. It was always the correct amount, as this was all she could really afford. She said; the beers were her treat for the week. What she ordered was a little small for the company to deliver, but the manager knew who she was and allowed it. Lying on the table, beside the money for the beers, was a small amount of coins, amounting to around thirty or forty pence, which she had put there for my tip, which, in those days I thought was quite a considerable amount as a tip, especially, as this old lady was a pensioner, blind and had very little. She would always ask me if I wanted to drink something myself, and I always declined, as I did not want to take advantage and I was so busy trying to finish the round before the weekend. I also used to refuse the tip, but she always insisted I took it. As the old lady was blind, she would work out how much to give me beforehand, by feeling the money with her hands. For this, I was so grateful and overwhelmed. Not because of the amount of money, but because this person had so little in the material way yet gave so much. She gave from her heart and the energy which she gave out by doing this every Friday afternoon, I would never forget. This person could teach us so much.

The same afternoon on my round, I would drive a little further on to a very large house in Millionaires' Road. There I used to deliver three or four crates of returnable glass bottles of soda siphons, two crates of lemonades, other soft drinks and some bottles of wine. This was a weekly delivery. On many occasions, the empty bottles were not returned and had been left in the garage to gather dust and cobwebs leaving me to have to crawl under a half opened garage, drag them out, put them in crates and load them into the van.

I appreciate this was part of my job but they made it very difficult for me at times, especially as I had a large delivery round and always came home late on Fridays, and with low pay. This was fine, but what really made me think and left me feeling a little empty one day after visiting the old lady was, when I had collected and loaded up all the dirty empties from this large house, instructed by the lady who owned it, her husband drove into the driveway in his new Rolls Royce, and called me over. He asked me if I had five pence. I searched my pocket and said 'yes'. The owner of the house then asked me to give it to him. I was a little confused at the time as to the reason why! Still I gave him the five pence and in return he gave me ten pence. I was shocked and speechless. It would have been better for him not to have given me anything at all.

There was this little old blind lady, giving everything from her heart, after I had only delivered two or three small bottles of Guinness to her, which was her weekly treat, and at the other end of the scale living in opulence was someone who was calculating every penny.

Phase Four

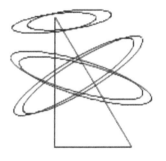

Being in the Present Moment

Phase Four

Being in the Present Moment

Being in the Present Moment

There are great changes coming now in this world. I sincerely hope the greed will lessen and we will all learn to speak from our hearts.

This is a time for new beginnings and great changes are happening around us. Of course not all will be to our liking and there will be many more disruptions and eruptions creating chaos in the future, but if we can accept and allow the changes to happen in this world we will become greater beings and we will have a better understanding of one another. Allow the positive energy to embrace and feel the energy around you. Change is necessary, it is inevitable in order for us to progress and evolve.

We all have self power, and now is the time to use it, as great changes are now happening within a new vibrational shift, raising our levels of consciousness to a higher frequency of awareness and understanding.

Intention

It is important to be focused on your intentions and goals at all times. Know what your reasons are behind your intentions and keep them secret to prevent them being weakened by outside negative influences. Only

Now It Begins

tell likeminded people. Also know what your reasons are behind the intentions.

Dreams and Desires

Often our desires are dissipated through our fears and doubts about things that may never happen. We have all had many desires throughout our lives, strong feelings of wishing or wanting to achieve something. Often we have diluted these desires because there is no support behind them or meaning, purpose or, simply, thought. Your dreams and desires will not manifest if there is no purpose or meaning behind them. You can create anything you desire, but in doing this, you must be careful how you go about it, as this can affect everything around us. So it is important the things you want most come from being focused and your desires have a true purpose.

We can change the world through our thoughts. In reality, there is no need for suffering on this earth. There is plenty for all of us. The answer to all suffering lies within the balance we create within our lives...

...whatever our desires may be

Honesty

Being honest with yourself in whatever it is you want is important. When we are not being honest with ourselves or others, we are only cheating ourselves.

The truth has greater power than lies

Forgiveness

This is an essential part within us for moving on in life. When we forgive others we are forgiving ourselves. When we forgive truly from our hearts and not just from our heads we free ourselves from being stuck in the past. We release a heavy burden that may have been with us for a long time. If we are unable to forgive, then this can turn from anger to bitterness, into hatred, guilt and illnesses. Through unconditional love and by not blaming others or ourselves for the mistakes of the past we become greater human beings with a greater understanding of ourselves and others. We are able to go beyond the ego and the pride that holds us back from our future progression and for all the things that we truly do deserve. If we could all learn to forgive unconditionally, we could change the world.

An Exercise for Forgiveness

This is to empower you to forgive yourself and/or someone else, whether they are living or have passed.

Find a quiet, relaxing place where you will not be disturbed.

Now It Begins

Lift, then hunch your shoulders for a moment and relax. Do this three times, and every time you hunch them up and let them go, feel yourself relaxing more each time.

Take a deep breath, hold it for the count of three and then relax. Every time allow yourself to sink deeper and deeper within yourself. Again take a nice deep breath, hold it and then relax letting all the tension flow out, leaving all the cares behind.

After reading the following passage, you may need to close your eyes to visualise.

If it is you who needs to forgive another and you are unable to do this by meeting them in person then see them in your mind's eye, no matter where this person or soul may be and send out unconditional love to them. If you cannot see them, feel their energy. Now imagine a beautiful glowing white light and send it out into the universe towards this person and surround them with it. When you have done this, tell them you forgive them from your heart, whatever has happened. Say anything else you feel you need to say, that was not said before. Do this now. Ask for their forgiveness too. As you send out the love, it will return when you are truly ready to forgive. You may need to do this more than once. If it is you, who needs forgiving, then ask for the other person's forgiveness with the same procedure.

Now It Begins

When you finally feel you have said all you possibly can, surround yourself with a glowing pink healing light. See, and feel yourself, being soaked in this warm light. Now direct this light to and around your heart area and forgive yourself for anything you may feel needs forgiving and let go.

Deserve

Sometimes we feel we do not deserve the things we should be entitled to in our lives. This mainly comes from negative suggestions we have received from others since childhood into adulthood. Whatever the reasons may be; our background, religion, and from what we have learned, we do deserve. Believe you deserve all the good things life has to offer and believe you already have it.

You do deserve whatever it is you may wish for no matter how you have been brought up in this world and no matter how you have suffered or whatever negative patterns of conditioning and emotions have been indoctrinated into you.

You do deserve! Those who have told you otherwise have told you through their own ignorance, jealousy, greed and the desire to control others.

It is very important not only to believe we will receive the things we want, but to believe we do deserve them, and to also believe in ourselves.

Now It Begins

When you are happy with yourself in the present you are creating happiness for your future.

Phase Five

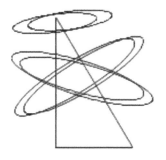

Feeling Good
About Yourself

Phase Five

Feeling Good About Yourself

Feeling Good About Yourself

Why do we need to feel good about ourselves?

When we feel good we open up endless possibilities for ourselves and others. We raise our vibrations to a higher frequency, being open to all things possible, giving us greater strength in our beliefs and increasing the chances of achieving the things we want in life.

Feeling good about ourselves can change the molecular structure within our bodies and create better health. It can make us look and feel younger, just as laughter can improve health and create longevity. In India, there are places where people gather together early in the morning for the very purpose of laughter. When we have a smile on our face this in turn, will cause others to smile and feel good about themselves, as we are all reflections of each other. When we feel good about ourselves, we are processing our thoughts and anchoring them with our feelings, this helps us to be grounded.

Good feelings combined with unconditional love is everything!

Now It Begins

When we are able to love ourselves and others unconditionally all things are possible. This is one stage further towards our personal progression.

You can feel good by being in the present moment. Often when negative things happen in our lives, it can cause our thoughts to wander, creating worry and anxiety about the future, or regrets from the past. When this happens, focus your mind on the present moment and send those negative thoughts away.

Take a couple of deep breaths and feel good about yourself. Practise this throughout the day.

You might visualise in your mind a favourite place, like a beach scene with beautiful white sand and turquoise sea with palm trees, or a beautiful garden, with flowers and trees everywhere. Play your favourite music, or watch something funny on TV. Anything, in fact, which will make you feel good about yourself.

Create affirmations to say out loud, expressing gratitude for what you have now and for all the good things that are coming to you. Feel them and believe that you have them already.

Processing positive thoughts and anchoring them to our feelings is an essential part of realising the things we want. Our thoughts alone will not hold the power to attract the things we desire. Once we have felt

Now ItBegins

what it is we desire then we can attract it. So it all comes down to how we really feel about ourselves, and what we feel we deserve. If you do not believe and really feel you do not deserve what you are asking for then it will not happen. Our feelings inside are so important.

How can we explain certain things without experiencing the feelings first? For example; what a certain fruit may taste like. The best way to describe an orange would come from something we have already experienced. The citrus taste of how juicy it might be, bitter or sweet. We can best describe things through our feelings. This is why it is important to process our thoughts through to our feelings. Once we have felt it, then we can anchor those feelings, providing they are relevant to what we want to keep and serve a purpose in our lives. If they do not, learn from the experience and let them go, do not hold on to them. By doing this, we are able to keep what we want with us for as long as necessary or for as long as we wish. Through our feelings we create and manifest.

What are your true feelings? Notice what you are feeling right now or, when your moods change, as we all have many different moods throughout the day. Are they feelings of anger or calmness, happiness or sadness, sorrow or depression, or are they spiritual? Some feelings may predominate over others until we have a greater understanding of them. Learn to know the reasons why you feel the way you do. Get in

Now It Begins

touch with your feelings. By doing this you will have the answers for the things you need to know, because there are reasons for everything!

Do not suppress any feelings, allow them to come to the surface, deal with them and then let them go. All the hurts from our past may still be buried deep in our unconscious minds. They may occasionally enter into the conscious mind, sometimes bringing up uncomfortable feelings through emotions of anger or sadness. Ask yourself where these emotions have come from. Often, if the emotions are too great, they may get trapped when we are not ready to release them. This will then need work. Once again, it is about facing your fears, dealing with them and letting go. Know what you are feeling. This is also the same with ailments and illnesses of the body, listen to your feelings of your body, to what it is telling you. You can be the best judge of your body when you listen from within.

Health and Healing

One day we may all learn to heal ourselves as we are now changing our thought patterns and vibrations towards thinking this way. In the past, western medicine has served a great purpose, and still does, yet, we as individuals as well as those in the medical profession are now looking for alternative cures and answers to solve the problems of modern diseases. Many now are using a 'holistic approach' in the hope for cures after becoming disillusioned with taking the synthetic prescribed drugs which have been offered in the past, and with long term use may create more severe illnesses and emotional problems, leading to depression and even suicidal tendencies. After a length of time our bodies build up a resistance and tolerance to these drugs and eventually, they have less effect towards serving their purpose. In many cases, of course it is necessary to take the medicines provided as they can help or at least suppress illnesses and as yet, an alternative cure may not have been found. However, the overuse of most drugs will create a harmful amount of toxicity in the body which can become fatal. Someone once said; 'We do not die of old age, we die of toxicity.' Western medicine has its place and has worked wonders in saving people's lives but it treats the symptom of the illness at the time and not the cause. An holistic approach and the ways in which many in the Eastern world work, are to find the causes from within. In this way, it is also treating and releasing our emotional blockages at the time of healing.

Many ailments and illnesses develop through our mental and emotional state and are transferred eventually entering into the physical body. In fact, we are vulnerable even before they reach the mental and emotional parts, entering and penetrating through our aura. The aura is an energy field which surrounds our bodies; as everything consists of energy. It is a shield invisible to the human eye, although, some who are trained in this can see auras, the colours and the energy which surrounds them and gives us protection. Auras can also be seen through special cameras and equipment, scientists are constantly working on this so they may learn and understand more.

When our aura is weakened or pierced with holes it can leak, leaving us open to negative energy or entering our physical bodies. For this reason, it is so important to have good thoughts and a healthy mind, to strengthen our energy force outside of the body and from within. Following this, the body will take care of itself, or in a true sense, the mind takes care of the body. This has a two way connection and yet it is all from one source. We have many external layers of subtle energy, bodies surrounding the physical body and the etheric which is the layer of the body related to the aura.

When we are feeling low in energy, we are more likely to attract a virus or illness as our aura is weakened, especially if our energy source is allowed to be run down continually like a car battery, with a feeling of being totally drained with little life left in it. Everything needs recharging occasionally, just like we all need a good rest or a change from our normal routine.

An illness can develop for many years before certain physical signs may be noticed. Often, when the symptoms have shown themselves to appear in the physical body, we will seek medical advice. As the causes may not have been recognised and possibly

Now It Begins

been lying there dormant for a long time, sometimes it may be too late for a cure or even to suppress the symptom or illness.

The medical profession can only deal with what they have been taught and what is written in their journals. They cannot work miracles, yet they are doing their best to perform whatever they can do and with so many new strains of viruses and illnesses they have a great deal to cope with. This is why it is now time to look within and start helping ourselves, creating good health and longevity. It is a good time to look back at natural medicines, traditions and cures that have existed for thousands of years. Now it is time to reconstruct and learn from our past.

Stress

One of the biggest threats to humans among other things is stress. Stress has been around since time began, it has always existed even within animals, but modern day stress is prolonged. Long term stress is damaging and can eventually cause severe illness or death. This again, relates to our emotional well being.

I guess, I have had to learn this lesson many times over, maybe some of us never really learn it when we trust and give too much. After one incident, we lost our home and owed a large sum of money to the bank. We had other negative things happening around us that I had attracted unknowingly so I was

Now It Begins

actually pleased to walk away from it all, as we were now free from a stressful business.

As a result of all the stress, and being quite a sensitive person, I contracted a neurological virus between the neck and the brain, an inflammation of the nervous system.

I returned to see another consultant four years after the first diagnosis. Seeing my medical notes, he asked me what the problem was, in a very disinterested tone of voice. I lost interest in asking for help and started to work on myself. Gradually I had to let go of the things that were no longer good for my body and state of mind.

Over the years I have changed my life a great deal and I am still working on myself to create internal balance. Possibly if I had not done so, I feel I may have deteriorated rapidly. I blame no-one for this because it was through my own making and experience. I also feel my problem originated from my childhood, in which my emotions were suppressed.

We all have our Achilles heel. Learn yours and create a balance within. Listen to your body, as quite often, you will be notified by pain, this is a great beacon towards showing us something which may be not quite right! Of course, many illnesses are also genetic, but we can still change our thought

Now It Begins

processes, and life styles, which eventually may create well-being within our bodies.

As for some like myself, we may be stronger in the spiritual sense or in the creative world and for those who are like this; we do not usually work well under stress. Everything has its time and you know when you may have reached a limit to what you can do or, when one is overloading, how to avoid blowing a fuse.

Many people say they cannot find the time to relax. This is an excuse; we all need to make time for ourselves to learn how to relax - how can we help others if we are not relaxed ourselves? It has now come to the stage in these modern stressful times when we all need to find ways to relax.

Relaxation Therapies

I have given many people therapy from all walks of life and for a variety of reasons and as the world is changing so fast it seems many are becoming more stressed in both their professional and personal lives. Those to whom I have given therapy have all been stressed to a high level of anxiety.

At first, in the early stage of the session when giving hypnotherapy to these clients, they will often resist relaxation. This may be due to the kind of work they practise, needing to be so precise and in control, leaving very little room for relaxation. After a certain amount of time has passed the client becomes relaxed and gradually goes into a deeper state of trance, in which they are completely in control and aware of what is happening. By this time, with their permission, I am able to gain access through their unconscious mind and they are then open to receiving positive suggestions. This can have an amazing effect and great benefits that may help the person in many ways. By the time I bring them back to the conscious state of mind, with their eyes open, they are in a total state of relaxation, a little sleepy, but totally relaxed and feeling good about themselves, with high self esteem and confidence. Of course, sometimes further sessions are required depending on the individual and issue but one session can have an amazing effect.

After the client has regained their state of consciousness, I will show them techniques for how to relax, with breathing and self hypnosis so they may use it in their own time. I will also instruct the client on giving themselves positive affirmations during this process.

It is now time to change our ways, so we may learn how to help ourselves in order to help others in a much more relaxed and positive way. When those who are in the professions of helping others are relaxed, those who need their services will also feel more relaxed. In this way the client/patient receives a greater level of healing and will benefit more.

Now It Begins

Healing

I sincerely hope one day it will be compulsory for all nurses and others who are involved in the medical profession to take a healing course, so they may give and receive healing to themselves and to their patients. Healing can also be given in an unconscious way, just by feeling good about ourselves and sharing this energy. In other words, not just working through the conscious thought from the conditionings of what we have been taught in our past, but a little from our heart when it is required can prove to be really beneficial.

Reiki (pronounced 'Ray-Ki') is a laying on of hands, energy healing technique, and is thought to be thousands of years old. It is a Japanese word, 'Rei,' meaning 'Universal Spirit,' and 'Ki,' which means - 'Life force.'   These words are thought to have originated from 'Raku-Kei.'   Raku is the vertical energy flow and Ki is the horizontal flow of energy flowing through the body. Therefore, the word Reiki refers to the balance of a universal and life force energy. Because of this balance, it will somehow give the correct amount of energy required when used in healing and will naturally find its way to the areas where it is most needed, without the practitioner having to give any direction.

It is based on the ancient wisdom and sacred symbols of Tibetan Buddhist monks and was rediscovered in

Now It Begins

the late 1800`s by Dr Mikao Usui Sensei, a Japanese Buddhist. The system of Reiki is a very simple yet powerful form of healing which can be given, received, and easily learned by anyone.

Besides the potential of healing the body, it can lead one to go beyond the ego and see 'Reality."

I have taught and given Reiki healing to many people from different religions and cultural backgrounds and I am pleased to say; with the majority of those who have learned this healing technique, it has changed their lives for the better, many have gone on to create a new future for themselves, as well as helping others. The few to whom it did not make a difference in their lives were possibly not ready for the changes at the time. However, when the seed is planted, it will often grow, even if it takes a little more time. We can only change our ways and life when we are ready and not before, and obviously, when we want to change.

Healing is universal. It holds no boundaries regardless of our differences in beliefs. It is energy from one source and we can all connect to it with amazing results. Also those who have received Reiki healing have found it has helped them in many ways. There is no guarantee for any type of healing but, miraculous cures have been witnessed by many over time. I have seen it, even with distant healing when given to others. As well as healing ailments and illnesses, Reiki is also great for stress reduction. I always say to those who are interested in Reiki, there would be less

Now It Begins

violence and wars in this world if we all learned Reiki or any other form of healing. This can only promote positivity and altruism in a world that needs healing and can and will do no harm, if taught and given in the correct way.

Teach your children the art of healing and they will show you a new world of change.

Treatment

A Reiki treatment works by dissolving or releasing toxins through the vibrations which take place on a higher frequency of one's being, whether it is on the physical, emotional, mental or spiritual level. Creating a harmonious environment from within ones self.

When giving Reiki, it does not matter if it is a person, a pet, a plant or an object, the energy will flow into it.

When I am teaching or giving Reiki healing or hypnotherapy to others, I show how to become grounded. Being grounded can be likened to an electrical cord which is earthed. Grounding can be very important, especially when someone is feeling a little disoriented. It is the same for humans, when we are earthed, we are grounded, and we are connected to the earth's energy!

This is a simple technique, by using our legs and deep breathing.

Now It Begins

Some Basic Grounding Techniques

With this exercise; it is better to remove shoes and socks, so you may feel the earth's energy. Sit down at home or work, place both feet firmly on the ground and push down. Hold the position for a few seconds. As you do this, you are tensing the muscles in your legs and feet, connecting your spine and body with the flow of energy to ground yourself.

After you have done this, allow yourself to relax and take a slow, deep breath in and slowly breathe out. Follow this procedure a few times. This is grounding your body and connecting you with the earth. You are connecting with the earth and its vibrations.

Another exercise that can be done when sitting, or standing if you prefer, is to imagine roots from a tree coming up from the ground and attaching themselves to your feet and ankles, and as this is happening, feel them pulling you into the ground. You are being firmly rooted, feel yourself sinking into the chair if you are sitting. When you have done this, again, take some deep breaths, relax and feel the energy entering from below, grounding you.

The Importance of Thought

Dr Masaru Emoto is a Japanese scientist who has experimented with water and energy. He is renowned for some amazing discoveries.

Now It Begins

One of his experiments was to take some water droplets and separate them. He played classical music to one droplet and to another droplet he played heavy metal music. After this, he froze the water droplets and then placed them under a microscope. The results were amazing; the water droplets that were exposed to classical music had revealed a beautiful bright clear crystal formation in the shape of a star. The droplet that was exposed to the heavy metal music showed a dull grey spiral shaped crystal that almost looked like a whirlpool.

He also experimented with two jars, which he filled with cooked rice and sealed each one. He separated both of the jars and wrote 'I Love you' on the first jar on the left and the second jar on the right, he wrote 'You Fool'. He spoke these words to each jar for thirty days. He then asked school children to say these words out loud to each jar, every day for thirty days.

At the end of thirty days, the rice in the jar on which he had written 'I love you' was still white in colour and looking quite fresh. However, the rice in the jar on the right side was almost black and looked totally inedible.

It has also been shown when samples of water were taken from Lourdes, a holy place in France, and placed under a microscope, a beautiful, bright star shaped crystal formation was revealed under the microscope.

Now It Begins

Through prayer also, many people gathered around water of a lake that was unsuitable for human consumption. After the concentration of thought through prayer the water had been cleansed and purified.

It may seem the answers here are possibly to do with memory, because memory is contained within all living things in the universe and in this world, within trees, plants and flowers, animals and every cell in our bodies.

The body's immune system fights off diseases with the help of memory cells, which defend against bacteria or viruses and learn to adapt or change if an infection should try and re-enter. This may be why it is said you cannot catch the same cold or strain of virus more than once, although there are many different variations of the same virus.

There have been many accounts of people, after receiving transplants of organs from donors, having developed cravings or have taken up different sports or habits only to discover later the donor also had the same traits. The information seems to be transferred from the donor to the recipient. Has energy been stored and transferred from the organ? Or is it of a more spiritual nature where the deceased person possibly has not let go of the world they have left and are still attached to the organ or to the person who has received it, as many donors do die of unnatural causes. This again, all seems to relate to memory.

Now It Begins

Then, there is past life regression; a memory which has existed before!

When we use certain thoughts and words they can change the molecular structure of our bodies. So, our choice of words is very important.

Once again I say; be aware of how and what you think, as even the words you speak will affect your whole being and everything around you.

Just imagine how your thoughts are affecting your own body!

Be kind to yourself as you can now see how thoughts can heal.

We are shaping our future as we speak, and the worldaround us.

Phase Six

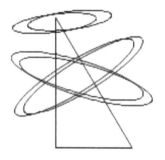

Being Content

Phase Six

Being Content

Contentment

Most people do not know what they want. We are
always searching for something within our lives and

Now It Begins

never being quite content with what we already have and sometimes not even recognising what it is we do have.

Being content is the greatest thing. It is something which cannot be bought. Contentment is a feeling that comes from within, an inner peace of mind engendering happiness.

Contentment comes from acceptance of who we are and where we are at this present moment in time. It is cherishing the moment, but at the same time allowing it to pass when something else may take its place. Appreciating each moment in time, for whatever it may be. No matter how long it lasts, as nothing is permanent in life. Everything changes within each cycle.

When I am working as a professional palmist, many people are surprised when I tell them the lines on the hands can, and do, change as little as between two to three months, depending on what is going on within one's life. Everything changes, yet imagine what it would be like if things remained the same. Life would not only become very boring, but everything would stagnate as change is necessary for all living things to grow, to become fruitful and then to make room for the new creations in life.

We will always desire something in life. It would be difficult not to want things, as our desires give us pleasure, though it is only a temporary pleasure in the main. Yet, there are many things in life, which when we do receive what we have wanted may have taken such a long time, we no longer appreciate them, or no longer need what it was we had wanted before. Yet there are many times when we get what we want, and find we no longer want it.

This is because our lives have changed, we have moved on. The more we become aware of ourselves and our surroundings, the more we realise we need less in our lives. We come to understand whatever we receive and take on in life, the greater our responsibilities become. For most of us, as we age, we are seeking fewer responsibilities for those things that create heavy burdens in our lives.

We are often seeking the opposite, relaxation and contentment. There are, of course, those who have great ambitions in life and continue to seek challenges until their last days on earth. This is what they want; it is what motivates them. Perhaps they have found a true purpose in life, or maybe they are still searching for something which they themselves have not yet found.

Remember, whatever it is you may be searching for; the answer will always lie within. The reason all things can be created and work together with our intentions, is because we are all made up of the same thing, energy. We are all connected to the one source, the universe, and the universe is connected to us, with each vibrational frequency that is sent out.

When changes are imminent on a global scale, we eventually move towards the level of accepting it and understanding what a great change has occurred and why.

We can only take on what we are ready for at the time and no more. We can also make changes happen in this world and this will affect the changes within ourselves.

Wherever your true purpose may be, it is necessary for it to always come from within. Know what your intentions are. Life should be kept as simple as possible so we may enjoy it. True happiness can only come from contentment, which comes from within.

There is a great story, not sure exactly of its origins, and this may be a slight variation. A business man takes a holiday and travels around the world. He arrives in India and spends some time in a small fishing village along the coast. There, he meets a poor humble fisherman, who goes out every day on his boat and casts his net for the fish he can sell at the market on his return.

One day the businessman said to the fisherman; "If you spent more time, worked harder and took a loan

Now It Begins

out, you could buy another boat and have someone working for you."

The fisherman replied "What would be the point of that?"

"Well, then you could pay off the loan and eventually buy another boat."

"What would be the point of that?" asked the fisherman again.

"Well then you could have more people working for you and then buy a fleet of boats," answered the businessman.

Once again the fisherman asked "What would be the point of that?"

"Well," said the businessman "you could have enough money eventually, to buy a bigger house."

Again the reply came: "What would be the point of that?"

The businessman said finally; "Then one day you can retire, take a boat out, relax, and do some fishing."

Sometimes we may not appreciate the things we already have.

Now It Begins

Having travelled to many beautiful places in this world, I have noticed there are always those who are not happy with what they have, even though their surroundings are so beautiful. Understandably, they have to survive and may have heard stories about where they can make more money or have a better lifestyle in certain other places or countries, and this may be true, but there is always a price to pay. The grass may appear greener on the other side but the illusion can soon fade in experiencing the reality.

There is one group of people among others for whom I have always had great respect and admiration when meeting and speaking with them in India and Nepal and these are the Tibetans. Despite being driven into exile from their homes in Tibet after fleeing from the Chinese invasions with their leader, his holiness the

Now It Begins

Dalai Lama, these people have remained humble after so much suffering. Possibly, they gain their strength from their beliefs in Buddhism and spirituality. We can all learn from these people and other cultures around the world who have suffered a great deal in the past. Surely, it is now time for us all to search our hearts for forgiveness and understanding, creating a balance and letting go of the old world of greed and a desire for control.

Unfortunately, there are still many in power that resist change, and will not recognise people like the Tibetans. It is sad that many of us will go through much suffering before finding contentment within.

Mahatma Gandhi said:

"An eye for an eye will only leave the world blind."

By creating a greater awareness and learning to appreciate what we have, we can become more content, no matter where we may be at this present moment in time on earth.

When we learn to love ourselves, we will unconditionally love others, and in turn love will come back to us.

Many of us find it hard to like and love ourselves unconditionally. This may be because we were not taught in this way. It can result in low self esteem, taking away our confidence.

'Now' believe in your hearts that the cold past of suppression, blame or guilt, has been lifted and we are now being shown new ways of understanding each other.

We can release the heavy burdens from our past as we are now moving into a new dimension of light.

Belief

A belief is something which we hold to be true, in whatever form it may exist or not. It is an acceptance often of something which we cannot prove exists. Yet, through our beliefs all things can be achieved and are created. We have the power to create through our beliefs. When we believe in a God, Goddess or a powerful universal source of light and energy, we give it a greater power to exist within our lives. Just as we do with dark energy. When there is no belief in the source, it may cease to exist from within our lives. Often our beliefs can and do change. Sometimes when something dramatic happens in our lives we may no longer believe in the things we once held so true to our hearts. There are also those who may never have believed in the intangible and then something happens to them, which has such an

Now ItBegins

impact that it changes their lives forever. This gives them the opportunity for greater openness and belief in something greater than themselves. To everything there is a purpose even though we may not know it at the time.

As the old saying goes 'You will not find an atheist on the battle field.' We may all pray for something in times of desperation whether we believe or not.

Everyone believes in something, even non-belief is some form of belief.

We are simply humans, should we be so arrogant to think nothing greater exists besides ourselves? When we become too egotistical, there will always be something to put us in our place, bringing us back down to earth, sometimes with a bang. Although this does not mean we cannot achieve great things. It just means, we need to be aware of what we do and how we achieve it, as what goes out, returns.

On this earth, we are all only a part of the jigsaw of the things we are working on and if anything, a tiny squiggle in this one giant universe.

When we believe in our higher selves, we become one with a universal energy of light, giving us a greater purpose to exist within ourselves and knowing all things work together from one source, as we are one.

Now It Begins

This is where it all begins, as well as; having the belief within ourselves, believing and having faith in something which we cannot see.

It comes down to our belief system, the way we have been taught, brought up, our background, our culture, our religion, and the way we have been conditioned from the past.

Whatever has happened in our lives up to now has resulted from our past.

Only when we are flexible and become less opinionated and non-judgemental, can we change our beliefs and outlook on life, so we are able to see things from different perspectives.

If you are confused in any way about your life or beliefs, detach yourself from whatever is causing the confusion for a while.

When you disassociate yourself from the attachment or attachments you have made in your life, you will find it easier to see a clearer and bigger picture of what is happening around you, even if it is a temporary detachment. After you have done this, you may also know what is true and you can then act upon whatever may be necessary at the time.

Listen to your inner self for the answers.

Now It Begins

No matter what you believe in, you do have choice.

There is no right or wrong path, the path which you have chosen is the right one for you at this moment in time.

Do not allow other people's negativity to influence you, believe and allow the universe to do its work for you.

Young people often visit me asking for advice when I am reading palms in public. Some of them are very confused because of their religious backgrounds and parental influence. Often, couples will come to me wanting to be together, but the customs of their families and religions do not allow two different cultures to marry, or sometimes they may be gay, a taboo in many cultures.

It is very difficult for me to give guidance without feeling as if I am interfering. I will tell them they must respect their parents but it is their lives they must live. It is their choice and they must make it. In life, it is our purpose to help, guide and show others the way, not to control them

This is now the time to remember who we are and what we have been given in this life. It is a time to free ourselves from the restrictions which we may have learned and been conditioned to from our past; a time for equal balance and opportunities for one

Now It Begins

another; a time to share and communicate with each other.

Do not be afraid of change. Believe. Allow. Accept You Deserve It.

Phase Seven

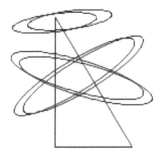

Sixth Sense

Phase Seven

Sixth Sense

Sixth Sense

Most of us are aware of our five senses and some will be aware of higher vibrations. By accepting and acknowledging there are more than the five senses, we will create a greater awareness of our higher selves.

Although there are actually another five senses beyond the physical level and possibly more in the higher realms of spiritual vibrations.

The sixth sense is intuition.

There are many frequencies that exist beyond our senses which we are possibly unaware of, but they do exist. We all use our five major senses throughout the day and night; seeing, hearing, smelling, tasting and feeling, the sixth sense being intuition. Most of us will predominantly use one or two of the senses more frequently, for example; some of us will be visual (seeing), others will be auditory (hearing) and some could be more kinaesthetic (feeling).

This means those who are quite visual may focus on certain things by using their imagination to see images or words when trying to spell something. Those who may possibly be using auditory in a predominant way could mean they relate to hearing more often. Maybe they are a musician or a linguist. They may reply to someone when in a conversation by saying; 'Yes, I hear what you are saying'. Just as the visual person may say; 'I see what you mean', these people can often make good teachers.

Those that are kinaesthetic will be more in touch with their feelings. They may say 'I can feel it'. These people make good counsellors and certain therapists, such as healers, because they use touch, and are often in tune with them. Of course, there is the sense of smell (olfactory) and taste (gustatory), that some may use more often, possibly someone like a chef or a wine taster who relies on these senses.

Intuition

Finally, this brings us to the sixth sense, which is intuition. We all have intuition and do use it from time to time whether we know it or not. Some are more adept in using their intuition because they have become aware of it at some stage in their lives; it may be hereditary, passed on from our ancestors. If the family has kept in touch with its spiritual side, then it will possibly be inherited from a very early age.

We all have hunches from time to time, this is intuition. By using this sixth sense it can give us access to so much more, as we become more aware, by tuning into our higher selves and the great cosmos, bringing the things we want and need into our lives.

It is sometimes difficult to know if we are using our intuition or whether it is just a thought on a conscious level. The answer lies within; true intuition comes from our higher self. It comes from within, from above.

Many famous and successful business people use their intuition continually, and one of the reasons they are successful is because they do not allow outside influences to interfere with what they believe to be true. We all make mistakes, especially when using our intuition for guidance, as the conscious mind will make decisions and our unconscious mind can give us the inspiration. However, the more we are aware of our intuitive thoughts the more we will know what rings true and be able to act upon them.

So the next time you feel you may have a hunch or an inspired thought that may have come from out of nowhere, listen to what it is telling you.

One of the greatest ways to develop your intuition is through meditation. To know if your intuitive thoughts ring true you need to be in touch with your feelings, listen from your heart and not your head.

This will guide you to your true soul purpose and to know yourself from within. Intuition comes from your

Now It Begins

first inspired thought and creates a feeling, after which it may create confusion in the brain, especially when doubt enters in your mind and from outside influences. It may come in many forms; through our feelings by day or night, in dreams, listening to the inner voice, through images and physical sensations or even upon waking from sleep. So intuition can and does play a very important part in our lives, as we all have and use our intuition. Obviously, some of us have developed more than others, but you will be amazed what you find when you allow it to work for you. Using our higher senses is going beyond the mind, and there is nothing to be afraid of. At one time, we all had very strong intuition and used our sixth sense to a great extent. Many of us have lost the awareness of using our higher (and even lower senses for some), to a degree, through modern day life and having also been conditioned in the past to believing it can play no part in our everyday lives.

Centuries ago, we would have been burned as witches for even the mention of such things. The majority of those who were condemned to death were mainly all women and innocent children branded for using nature and their natural powers of the senses. In fact, executions are still taking place today in certain countries for what they may call sorcery. One person who has been recently condemned was just giving out predictions on satellite TV.

The ability to have natural talents has always been suppressed throughout the ages, even for those who were musicians and artists, and even now this continues in some countries.

The Esoteric and Religions

It is time once again to be open to something which is far greater than ever before. This is not Devil worshipping or an evil source, as some of certain backgrounds would still believe. No, this is a universal energy and it is our natural right to receive and deserve it, whatever you may have been taught.

It is all one source, and it is how you tap into it, which makes a difference.

Many people of different religious backgrounds have come to see me in the past. Often, they will say to me when being given readings in palmistry; 'I am not supposed to do this kind of thing, because my religion does not allow it, but I am very interested in how it works and need some help within my life'. I reassure them I am not performing witchcraft as some may do or, removing or casting spells. I am just here to give them guidance as to where they may already be going in their life. I tell them they already have all the resources within them and if they listen from within, they will know the answer.

The way in which I work with palmistry is rather like looking at a road map. For example, the surrounding edges of the palms could be seen as the mountains. In the centre are the valleys, the larger and deeper

Now It Begins

ones are motorways or main roads with shallower ones being the side and back roads. As we shape our own future we create and build new roads and the old ones fade and may no longer have a through route. Extending all this to a greater capacity I will use my intuition. This will happen often, sometimes I am aware of it and sometimes not.

I am a spiritual person and respect all religions, even though I believe there should be no separation between humankind, as this can slow our progression down towards evolving on a higher level of consciousness and creating understanding and sharing an unconditional love with each other on this earth. Neither do I wish to offend God, humans or those who may be a part of any religion. As I believe we are all of one source and are working together.

I have questioned my spiritual beliefs and views on different religions many times over the years, especially with regards to working within the esoteric field. Over the years, I have had born again Christians come to me when I have been working to tell me what I am doing is very wrong, and do I not care about being saved in the afterlife? Everyone has a point, and their belief, both of which I respect.

My conclusion is; if there are those of us who are doing our best towards helping others in the way in which we know how, and providing we are experienced in what we do and are causing no harm to others who have come for advice, some of whom

Now It Begins

may be suicidal and desperate with so many issues and problems and often do not know who else they can turn to. Are we doing wrong? I have faith and a spiritual belief in a universal creator or energy.

The separations that exist between humans is from an age old concept, which may have worked in the past and may have also been necessary, but this has also been contrived through asserting fear and manipulating the ordinary people which was used for political reasons of power, gain and control. Whatever you believe and wherever your faith may lie, only you can know the truth. You are your own Guru; and the master of your own destiny.

Our inner strength and wisdom can be compared to a fruit tree. The seeds you sow show who you are and your intentions. The roots of the tree are your inner strength and guidance which is a direct source to your soul and universal consciousness. Its trunk is your growth and stability. The branches are the divisions and separations of your journey in life. The final outcome of the tree will be the fruit it bears. You will learn and taste the sweetness or bitterness of its intentions.

Know your inner strength and the path you have chosen through altruism it will return wholly and magnify.

The time has now come where we must all learn to work together without separation.

Now ItBegins

Channelling

Whether it is with palmistry, psychic experiences, through my work with different therapies or writing this book, more often than not, I feel I am being guided from a higher source that often takes over, allowing my writing, words and healing to flow, giving me direction and answers . I also usually know when this is not happening because, I start to think hard of what to say or write about, this mainly happens when I am tired or when my energy is low, as the connection fades or is blocked. Many of you who tap into your creative or spiritual side will know this feeling. This in effect is channelling, being open to the higher source of energy and connecting. It is how clairvoyants, clairaudients and clairsentients work, although there are different levels of vibrations and frequencies which they may tune in to. Of course, with work that requires creativity, there will always be a certain amount of conscious effort required, especially if it is to be projected out into the world. As the saying goes -'one percent inspiration and ninety nine percent perspiration!'

Palmistry

I have always described palmistry as a skill and a science and using one's intuition, though not all of us use intuition.

I always tell my customers 'just use your awareness when going for a reading, listen to what feels true to your heart.' It is not a guessing game, or about holding back and blocking your energy, as many clients do to test the readers, when doing this, it can sometimes result in a very average reading because you may be cutting off your flow of energy. It is about receiving what you have come for and if the answers are to be revealed it will be so, providing the reader is experienced in their field. If you leave after a reading and feel good about yourself, then this may tell you quite a lot about yourself and the reader. However, use your intuition. When people just stand by the place where I am working and say to me; 'How do I know you are any good'? I reply; 'You don't, use your intuition!'

I have given readings to people and then seen them seek another reading of a different kind five minutes

Now ItBegins

later, somewhere else. This is fine, but some people will never be happy, often they are not listening to the true points of what I am telling them. Maybe they are just not ready to hear it. Often, depending on the reader, they will obtain the same or a similar answer to their questions elsewhere. The answers can sometimes lie hidden when the client is hoping for something big to be revealed, it might be the smallest of answers that are the most meaningful.

Some years ago a lady came to me for a palmistry reading and because of her issues of anxiety, I suggested I give her Reiki healing. The lady was stressed and had to take an anti depressant pill to travel to come and see me. When she arrived, I talked with her for a while and then proceeded with the healing. Reiki is very relaxing and some clients when lying on the therapy couch with soft music in the background and receiving the healing energy often fall asleep. This lady managed to talk all the way through.

It was obvious she needed to talk and I believe the Reiki did very little for her, or at least not on a conscious level.

After I had finished the healing, which was more like a counselling session, she made one statement which summed it all up. She said; 'Do you know I would be quite happy to be in therapy for the rest of my life.' I knew then she was not ready to move on in her life.

Now It Begins

She had made up her mind to remain being stuck in the past.

One day, we will all be very aware of our higher senses. We will communicate through speech and on a higher level with telepathy.

This has already began, as many of you will have had experiences of knowing who is at the calling end of the phone, or who is at the door before the bell may even ring. These are just very small examples of what the future holds for us all, especially for those who are showing willingness and openness to the higher self now, regardless of your previous thoughts or experience.

Animals have always used telepathy with humans and between themselves. They also know when things are about to happen. After the tsunami of 2004 over one hundred and fifty thousand people died. As far as I am aware there were few accounts of animals found dead.

I was in Thailand and Sri Lanka one month after it had happened, I could feel the sadness around, like a cloud of doom that hung over both countries. It was devastating and the damage which it had left was staggering and yet, it is amazing how all the animals escaped.

Animals are well in tune with their six senses and feel the vibrations on a much higher frequency than us humans do. Research has been shown by scientists, a

Now It Begins

toad had been known to leave his mating grounds five days before an earthquake had occurred and the day before it happened, the last toad had left.

Now It Begins

Children often use their intuition a great deal more because they are open to receiving the frequencies and intuitive thoughts. There are those children who are said to be known as; 'Indigo and crystal children'. Indigo children have been incarnating for many years now, they are here to show us how we can move on and evolve in this world. The crystal children are said to be of an even higher dimension. These children are now being born to show us the way forward. They know who they are and will know what their purpose is here on earth. I have met a few.

As we age and become adults, we often dismiss those instincts and no longer trust the messages and guidance that we receive. Women may often have and use their intuition more than men (though not always). The reasons can be because the pineal gland is accentuated more in females due to hormones. This gland is situated and lies behind the forehead in the brain and is connected with clairvoyance. The pituitary gland, which is situated a little lower than the pineal, also acts in this way. This gland is also connected to our psychic abilities. The pituitary gland controls growth and the endocrine system.

It has been proven with scientific research through meditation, stillness and calmness of the inner mind, we can develop our intuition. The more we practise, the more in tune we become and aligned within ourselves, thus, creating a greater awareness in achieving our goals and dreams.

Now It Begins

We are now being brought into a new world of change, raising our levels of vibrations, this is one of the reasons why it is time for us to be open, to learn and accept. Do not be left behind. We all need change from stagnation of the past. We are now being guided by others of a higher source with these changes, though only some of us will know by whom.

Coincidences/Synchronicities

Nothing happens by chance.

When people say; 'it was just a coincidence', there is so much more to it than just a coincidence. Yes, it is coinciding but for a reason. Everything is created for a reason and has a purpose; it is synchronicity with the universe.

I have always been aware of coincidences throughout my life, especially when travelling to other countries. A few years ago, I met a native North American Indian from Montreal, Canada. The first time I met him, we were in Delhi in India and then we saw him again the following year in Cambodia and then in Bangkok where he was selling CDs on his stall. The year after, we saw him in a restaurant in Goa near to where we were staying. Since then, we have not seen him again, who knows why these things happen! Although there is always a reason and I believe I know the answer to this one!

Now It Begins

We all attract to learn from one another, for there is always a purpose for the meeting. At the time, we may not always know the reasons why it occurred but often, when the connection for a purpose has been fulfilled, we will then move on. This connection may even go back through past lives, possibly some unfinished business we had with this person. Whatever the reasons, there is a connection, a purpose that we or the other person needs to receive.

As the Crow Flies

Some years ago, I was travelling with my partner Denize in the south of India through Kerala, which is a beautiful part of India with lush green trees of coconuts and backwater lakes. On this occasion we were travelling on a local bus. The bus was a bit of a bone shaker and lost its rear bumper a few miles back after hitting a bump in the road.

We were travelling with two British girls and a Canadian girl who was a journalist for the Toronto Star. We had met them in Kerala; the two British girls were making their way to the Hugging mother 'Amma', who literally hugs thousands of people, giving them all unconditional love and warm feelings. The two British girls were sitting with Denize on the back seat of the bus behind me, and I was sitting next to the Canadian girl, who was by the window.

Somehow I managed to get into the subject of ghosts and ghost stories, I do not remember what I was

Now It Begins

actually saying at the time, but the Canadian girl thought it was all quite spooky, even though she seemed to be listening intently and enjoying, to some extent, what I was saying.

She told me she had never really spoken about anything like this before, being quite a logical and down to earth person. I also had probably mentioned how superstitious people were in India.

The windows on the bus were very narrow and slightly open with horizontal bars going across them. So, there was little chance of anything going in or out of them. I cannot remember at what point it was as I was telling her a story, but I do remember it being quite significant, when suddenly, there was a loud bang at the side of the bus where we were sitting.

The girl next to me felt something flying over her head at a high speed, and shortly afterward something had struck me in the ear. At this stage, I had not seen anything. In between my legs I had placed a straw hat, that I normally wear to protect me from the heat. I could not believe my eyes; when I looked down and saw a very black, very large crow neatly placed, lying dead in my hat!

Quite amazing, it was a remote chance in millions this could have happened, and to land perfectly in the middle of my hat with the head and its tail sticking out. The crow must have hit the side of the bus, where the narrow opening of the window was and dropped in. It took me totally by surprise, and after looking down, I shouted; 'ahh'... and threw it up in the air and out of my hat.

Everybody else on the bus who was mainly local Indian people stared and looked back at me, wondering what was going on. At this point, the bus conductor came over and started to kick the big black crow out of the door. Denize, the other girls and I suddenly broke out into fits of laughter and we could not stop, some of the others on the bus, their faces turned from a very serious look to smiling and happy, and they also started to laugh. Eventually, everyone on the bus ended up in fits of laughter, not sure if they all knew what they were laughing at.

Does not everything happen for a reason?

Dreams and Visions in Sleep

What are dreams? According to Wikipedia; a dream is a succession of thoughts, images, sounds or emotions which pass through the mind during sleep.

There are many different types of dreams.

Through my dreams, I have had many premonitions over the years which have come true and most of these dreams have been so vivid I can remember them to this day. These dreams are unlike other dreams which occur every night (or day) when we sleep.

Now It Begins

Many will say they do not dream, actually we all dream possibly at least six times or more a night or early hours of the morning. However, not all dreams are prophetic. Some of us will have these types of dreams more than others. I have found my dreams come in waves, sometimes I will receive premonitions for two or three weeks and then they will stop and will not return for weeks, sometimes months. Some of these dreams have been revelations of things, which have happened on a wider scale and others within a closer environment with family, friends and other incidences which happened.

The only times when we may not dream of anything at all, is possibly when we are under the influence of alcohol or drugs. When this happens, we are not really sleeping, but are unconscious.

Our dreams are the outlets and escape routes to our everyday lives. They can guide us and show us where we are going in life. For those who accept the conscious mind more than the unconscious, our dreams are a great introduction into the unconscious mind and towards getting to know yourself.

Many years ago I used to keep a dream diary, and when I had a dream, I would manage to wake up in the early hours of the morning and write it down. The only problem is; each night I would have less sleep. In the mornings when I woke up, I would check my dreams out with a dream dictionary and look for the meanings. These days, I only write down the ones

Now It Begins

which I believe may be prophetic and, with practise, it has become easier to interpret all the dreams myself.

After a while, it becomes easier to know the difference between prophetic dreams which may come true within a certain period of time, and dreams which release information about the things which have been happening within our everyday lives.

Of course, there are other dreams which have potential meanings to them. Before you can know the difference between your dreams and the different meanings, you need to start looking into them. So, a good way to do this is, whenever you may remember a dream - write it down and then ask yourself what it might mean. By all means, buy a dream dictionary and look up the meanings. It can sometimes give useful answers. Although, if you listen carefully from within, you will receive the answers which will really guide you! Certain dreams that often repeat themselves more than three or four times during sleep, are more often than not telling you something is wrong, whether they repeat in one night or several nights. It can be showing you there is an issue or a problem, one which needs to be dealt with, in or around your life.

If you have come across this in your life, listen to what it is saying to you. Is the dream telling you to let go of something? Is it showing you that you need to face your fears? Just like the old monster in a dream which runs away or shrinks down to the size of

Now It Begins

a kitten when you have faced whatever it is you might have been worrying or fearful about. Through our dreams we can take control of our everyday lives, the two are working together, there is no separation. Dreams are the unconscious mind and our everyday lives are our conscious mind.

When I have dreams of a prophetic nature, I will normally dream them just before waking quite early in the morning, often at around seven o'clock. They are usually then revealed to me either on the same day of waking or within a few days. Although, for some people who have these kind of dreams, it may not be revealed to them until days, weeks, months or even years later. It depends on how far we project into the future. When we travel in our dreams to the astral plane all can be revealed. Some of us will recall having out of body experiences that can be known as astral travelling or projection. This is also very common when under medical anaesthetics during an operation; drugs can also create this state. Many have seen themselves above their body in the operating theatre. Some of you will also have experienced a feeling like falling in a dream state; this can be coming down and back to semi consciousness after astral travel.

Apart from prophetic dreams which I have had, I will sometimes wake between one or two hours after I have gone to sleep and will often see apparitions or whatever they may be, they are not always pleasant visits. However, they do disappear when I am fully conscious and awake. Strangely enough, I never remember having any dreams beforehand.

I would have put them down to images I may have projected through my mind from certain things which I may have seen or experienced in the recent days past in my everyday life. However, here is one account of the apparitions that I have witnessed;

The Story of the Goddess and the Temple

My story goes back to a few years ago, once again in India, Goa.

Now It Begins

My partner and I were staying on the second floor of an hotel. At the time, there were very few hotels around in this area, especially ones that were built above the first floor, as they were all small guest houses. It was a very basic hotel but, it had a small swimming pool (in India there is not much in between, it is either, below standards or above), it was also a convenient spot from where we could send some goods back as we had been travelling around India and were coming to the end of our trip.

On the first night of staying in the hotel, I woke up in the early hours, and to my surprise, sitting opposite me I saw an old woman. She was staring at me as though she was giving me the evil eye, if one could do such a thing and she was wearing an orange sash around her shoulder and waist. When I emerged from my semi conscious state, she faded and disappeared. As I have said; I never remembered any dreams before, and it is always as if my mind is blank. Yet, when I see anything on waking, it is as real to me, as anybody can be in everyday life. Often, I think there is a burglar standing in the bedroom.

It may have been one or two days later when it happened again, I went to sleep just past midnight, and at around an hour or so afterwards, I was woken up; to find a very tall young man standing there in front of me and looking up. He was dressed in white and was wearing sun glasses; he also had the orange sash over his shoulders and around his waist.

Now It Begins

I was thinking this was very strange, one character showing up is one thing and then another who is wearing sunglasses, it was becoming like a comedy show. Although at the time of the apparitions, I saw no funny side to it, it was quite scary, or at least the first visitor was.

So, another day passes and in the evening, or early morning I retired to bed, I fell asleep and after an hour or two had passed, once again, I was woken up; to find a young girl, holding a white flower and of course, wearing the orange sash!

This was all getting too much. In the past, I have experienced visions, but never ones which have been so closely associated with one another in a sequence like this.

The next day, I started to ask around the part where we were staying in Anjuna and received no replies from the local people, there was silence. In India people are very superstitious and most, would have probably not wanted to discuss this kind of thing, especially where we were staying, as I believe black magic did, or maybe still does exist in this area, as well as in others.

I was about to forget the whole thing, when a few days later, in the parcel office we were sending some goods back and I just happened to ask the young girl who worked there, and who was dealing with our

Now It Begins

goods if, she could shed any light on what had happened, as I strongly felt there was an answer to be found. Of course, I had to tread carefully, as some might think I was a little crazy!

Anyway, I mentioned it to her and to my surprise, she said; 'Well, I don't like to say; but, many years ago [not sure if it was meant to have been a few years ago or a few thousand], a temple was built not far from here.' She told us there was also a statue of a goddess which stood in the midst of this temple. Above the temple lived a wealthy man, who every day would spit, (as many people do in India), and every time he spat outside of his dwellings, it would land, not only on the temple but on the goddess. There was also a poor man who lived below, inside the temple, or beside it. Every day, he would see the rich man carrying out his act of spitting. This made the poor man very angry because it was showing disrespect. So he decided to place a curse on anyone who lived or stayed in a place higher than the temple, and within the vicinity which would have been somewhere around the second floor, where we were staying. I did hear another version; in which, the goddess herself had placed the curse. I am not sure if this story is symbolic or not.

It would be of great disrespect within most holy places around the world, to do something far less than spitting. This is what many of the locals believed, especially, if something was placed above

Now It Begins

which was polluting the temple. This idea is one which we do not share in the west.

This was possibly the reason why there were very few places to stay which were built on more than one level in that particular area. These days, as new people move in from other areas or countries with different beliefs and capitalistic ideas to build properties, these traditions often fade, although, the belief can still be found amongst the elderly and religious people.

The final piece to my puzzle came when I was driving along on a motorbike and noticed, not too far from where we were staying, the temple which the girl had spoken of, with the goddess, and around her was an orange sash. Another one solved!

Angels and Guardian Spirits

When using our intuition, we often have to be on the ball. Sometimes, very quick decisions need to be made and of course, it is far better to detach ourselves when we are faced with an awkward or dangerous situation. This is not always possible, as we may not have the time to stand and think about what we are going to do. There are usually three options when in a very tight spot and they are; fight, freeze (which is what many animals do) or flight. I have been in many situations over the years, some of which I would rather not have been in, and have

Now It Begins

luckily escaped them. Possibly, if I had not used my intuition, I would not be here writing this book. I have always felt and believed, like many of us do, that a guardian angel has always watched over me, especially in times of trouble.

Possibly, they guide us out of the danger at the time. Whenever I have had harrowing experiences to a degree of sometimes even losing a little faith to the possibilities of not getting through it, after it is over, I have felt a miracle has happened. Then I give praise and restore the faith I had lost. We are always being tested. One day, hopefully, I will pass, almost there!

Angels or our guardian spirits, may also give us the guidance at the time to use our intuition when it is possible in certain anxious situations.

There have been times when I have not been too sure if I have used my intuition or if it was a guardian angel that helped me, although I am sure they have both been present when I have needed help.

I remember a time when I was at the age of around thirteen. It was in the evening and I was playing with some other children. We were chasing each other and I was running along the top section of the Marylebone flyover, (the west way) which was the midpoint of the motor runway. It was at the early stages of development, just being built, and the road had not been laid, so I guess it was all pretty unstable,

Now It Begins

although not totally realising it at the time, being young, and also because it was covered over with plastic sheets. I remember running along it and suddenly, I heard a cracking sound, a wooden plank had broken underneath my feet which was used as a floor board and I went head first down, hit my head on another plank of wood below on a lower level, missing the concrete blocks which were everywhere and I eventually landed in a sand pit on my back, it had seemed like a very long time before I reached the ground. When I opened my eyes, another child was asking if I was ok; I replied; 'yes' feeling very dazed and a little sick as I was slightly concussed.

When I looked to see where I had landed, I noticed I was sitting very tightly squashed in, and leaning beside a large concrete stone block and in the middle of it was a large spiralled spiked iron rod which was cemented inside it. At the time of the fall, it was as if I was being guided to land in a safe place.

Many people have had certain experiences when they have been close to death, perhaps after an accident has happened and they have been left stranded somewhere alone in the middle of nowhere and no hope was in sight. An angel or a family member, who has passed away, has appeared before them. They have often seen a bright light around the angel or person, sometimes guiding them out of where they are, or there have been times when the person who is trapped there is rescued after seeing the angel!

Now It Begins

Others have also had near death experiences when they have seen light through a tunnel or religious figures, or family members beckoning them to go with them or towards the light. For those who have been able to speak about it, it has not been their time to depart.

It has been said we are all helped in whichever path we choose in life by our guardian spirits and by choosing to do good things in the world we will be helped continuously. Also if we choose to do so-called bad things in this world, we will also be helped. However, when we continue to follow the same path, we will eventually be helped by spirits with a negative influence who take over and will help us to continue on the journey towards destruction. This is the law of the universe, and it is of course, what we have often asked for!

Of course, none of us can say who would be helped and who would not be, it is not for us to say. There are many good people who have left this earth and may not have been helped in the way we are aware of, as there are many who have not done such good things and may have been helped. It is not for us to question, just like our time on this earth. Though, everything does have a purpose, it is not always for us to know what it may be, and if that is the case, then greater things exist in heaven above.

There have been different spirits that I have often felt the presence of and may have even seen a few around me at times in my life. I have, however, always been particularly drawn to a Native American Chief, Tatanka Yotanka, better known as Sitting Bull.

When I was a child, I would play cowboys and Indians and would always play the part of Sitting Bull.

In recent times clairvoyants have often sat opposite me when I have been giving readings and told me I have a Native American spirit over me and said the name of Sitting Bull.

Sitting Bull was one of the Lakota tribe and became Chief of the Sioux nation. He was a holy man and a medicine man and, yet, he was also a war chief and forced to defend the Sioux against the American army. Chief Sitting Bull had many premonitions. One of them was that he and his people would win a great victory. This came to pass at the Battle of Little Big Horn.

When I was in Ontario, Canada at a young age I stayed near an Indian reservation, Kettle Point on Lake Huron. I remember I was roller skating in the early evening when my friends said they had to go home. When I asked why, as it was still early, they said because of the Indians. I was a little shocked but they were fearful, believing that they all carried knives. I was not concerned and I think my friends thought this was because I was a part of the local Native American tribe.

Now ItBegins

I have a friend who lives in San Francisco and runs a psychic school for children and adults. He is a descendent of the Lakota tribe. I met him when he was in the UK giving demonstrations of psychic skills at a meeting. He approached me after the demonstrations and started speaking to me in the Lakota tongue. He thought I was from this tribe and was surprised to discover I was English.

So it may be that a strong Native American spirit is watching over me.

One never knows if intuition is sometimes needed or, a guardian angel.

This is the beginning of a new world of transformation and change. These changes have already begun and are gradually taking us to higher levels of understanding of ourselves and each other!

Phase Eight

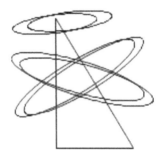

Cycles of Life

Phase Eight

Cycles of Life

Cycles of Life

A grandfather took his grandson to the lake and told the boy to pick a pebble up from the bank and throw it into the lake. As the pebble hit the water the grandfather said 'Focus on the ripple effect the pebble has created. Each ripple is a cycle of your life,' he explained. As the ripples expanded outwards and made a circle the grandson noticed the outer circle was coming towards him. The grandfather said to the child 'be careful what you cast out because everything will return to you at some point in your life.'

Now It Begins

All life exists within cycles. The universe and the planets in our solar system all have their own cycles which affect our lives. The earth has recycled and replenished at least four or five times previously. World events show cycles, our lives, our bodies, flora and fauna and in fact, all life on earth is created and ends within cycles.

Cycles create change and replenishment, they can show us when it is time to let go of what we may no longer need any more in our lives and also when new exciting things are about to take place within our lives. We may not always know when these are going to happen but many people will actually sense something and can become a little nervous or frustrated with their lives just before new changes are about to occur.

There are many cycles that do exist within our lives from the time of birth until we depart from this life and beyond. Each cycle is meaningful and will represent changes within our lives, some may last for a very short time and others can take years to pass through. For example there are three to four year cycles which are often apparent within people's lives. This cycle, as well as others, may show the highs and lows from the beginning to an end of whatever it is we may have attracted into our lives.

As the cycle begins; very positive and new exciting events may happen, or it could be a time in our lives, when certain things become more intense, bringing forward unresolved issues from the past, which can be very trying.

As it peaks in the middle and then slows down in the latter part, as nothing is permanent, no matter how trying or how wonderful things become, when the cycle eventually comes to an end, a new period will enter into our lives. Of course, it will depend on how effectively we deal with the situations we are involved in at the time, in order to free us from our past.

There is always a purpose to whatever may happen, and if within our lives there is a sudden downturn it can often be something which we may have created from our past and is now showing us something that we need to change before moving on.

Fashion, music and politics can also rise and fade within a three to four year period; making a statement against old ideas and beliefs and changing our culture as the younger generation take its place and strives for its independence with new and sometimes radical ideas. However, even the so-called new ideas may not necessarily be totally new as all things return and are recycled, creating little changes each time as we evolve into the next cycle.

We do have the ability to change things within our lives, being the masters of our own destiny to a certain extent but, there will always be times when things may become a little more difficult, as well as a little easier due to circumstances beyond our control.

Now It Begins

As the expression goes; 'Being in the right place at the right time', can sometimes make a great difference! In this world, timing can be everything, especially when we are waiting for something to happen or when wanting to attract certain things in our lives. It may be necessary; when wanting to attract the things we wish for, especially through our thoughts that it should be done only in the present time. It is also necessary to wait for the right time to receive. When we become impatient, we will simply push the things further away that we are trying to achieve. Plant the seeds, water them, but do not keep digging them up, allow them to grow!

It is also about how we deal with the opportunities which may arise in the present or future, as the way in which we have dealt with certain situations in the past will often be a reflection at some point in the future. The past will always present itself at some stage, just to let us know there may still be some unfinished business which you have not yet dealt with! This is the law of Karma.

As we enter into a new cycle, issues from the past which we may not have dealt with could show up, and obstacles may reappear from the time, similar to the last time they came around. For example; if you are entering a new twelve year cycle, and things may seem familiar from the past, like a feeling of déjà vu, then it could be certain things might be repeating themselves and showing up from twelve years past.

Now It Begins

In numerology; the number nine is quite significant, it can also be an end of a major cycle. When the cycle of nine years is complete, we may enter into a totally new phase. Many people have said to me in the past, that great changes often happen within their lives at around every ten years, bringing either chaos and disruption or new beginnings.

Again, we are a result of our past which can make a difference towards our future but, one reason for the changes occurring around every ten years could be that in numerology the number nine is a final number; after the count of nine it is reduced to a single digit, for example: $9+1=1$ which may indicate a new cycle after this time.

Numerology was very popular with early mathematicians and possibly dates back to around 10,000 years ago in ancient Egypt and Babylonia. It is still used today frequently in China and India. In Cantonese the number nine means: 'Long in time', 'enough'. There is also a link between numerology and astrology.

From birth, the seven year cycle can be very significant as many changes occur within it. The blood, cells and many other parts of the body including our emotions as well as the physical, can change and replenish during the seven year cycle.

The first seven years for a child are very important, shaping and creating their emotions, imagination, personality and characteristics. Over time, they enter into a new seven year cycle developing the conscious mind, learning to deal with every day issues in this world. As the saying goes; 'Give me the child until he is seven and I'll show you the man.'

The seven year cycle can also be very important within relationships. One major aspect I have noticed from giving readings to clients through palmistry, is if a relationship between two people is unstable and they have been together for slightly less, or more than seven years, fourteen or twenty one years and so on, within the seven year cycles, it can bring it to a climax.

The end results will obviously depend upon the couple and how they deal with the situations, but around the time of entering or leaving the cycle, the relationship will either become stronger, or it will weaken and the two, may well possibly part, depending what is at stake.

Entering into a new seven year cycle can also be a very positive time for the beginning of new relationships and meeting people. This can also be the same for those who have reached those ages mentioned before.

The seven year cycles play a very important part in our lives. From the first one; 1-7 years, to the seventh at 49 years of age and after which, it is all about the expansion of knowledge and acceptance with the world and our inner selves.

Now ItBegins

There are many cycles that may affect our lives which are governed by the planetary aspects of celestial bodies. Jupiter returns every twelve years to the place in your birth chart, where it was at the time you were born.

A twelve year cycle can be a time of expansion for travelling, education, career moves which can be prosperous and a time for developing spiritually.

Every twenty-nine and a half years from the time of birth, Saturn returns and is a time for teaching us discipline and patience, taking stock, possibly a time in one's life for slowing down a little and detaching, it may also be a good time for learning and studying. Whether we choose to believe or not, the planets can have great influence over the way we choose to live our lives. Everything is there to show us something, as we are all a reflection of the universe, the planets, the sky, the earth, the sea, ourselves and one another.

Each cycle brings about the different phases in our lives, what we need to learn before we can move on to our next destination. When a new cycle comes into our lives it may be a time to take stock and to discipline ourselves. It might be a time to move forward, meeting new people or to achieve and do the things which we have always wanted to, or a time to detach, relax and gain knowledge from within. When we detach ourselves from whatever we have been involved with, we are then able to see the bigger picture, and if we have not learned from whatever it is teaching us, we will simply repeat the lesson the next time another cycle comes around and re-enters our lives.

This may not always return in the same way we would imagine but, there will most surely be something there to show us about ourselves, some unfinished business if you like, that we had not learned from at the time and dealt with in the past. The answer lies in correcting our mistakes from the past by dealing with the issues in the present time. This is the same for our emotions, not allowing the hurts, animosity, jealousy, bitterness or resentment to build up, but to let go and to deal with the issues in the present.

The life cycle of a butterfly: the Egg - Chrysalis - Caterpillar - Butterfly

Now It Begins

The larger cycle that exists within our lives is of course; the duration of time spent on earth, from when we enter into this world until we finally depart.

However, there is one cycle which is even greater for those who may believe, and that is the cycle of; 'Re-Birth' or 'Reincarnation'.

We Have all Been Here Before.

I have been in psychic groups with guided meditations and there have been many times where I have travelled backwards in time into past lives. One life, which has been repeated in meditations, as mentioned before, is seeing myself as a Native American Indian.

In this vision the US cavalry is chasing me on horses. I know I am quite young and I am riding a brown and white horse bareback. The soldiers are quite far behind me, although I have come to the end of the path. I have reached the edge of the green grass on land. I stop, jump off my horse and stand alongside her. At this stage, I am not sure what to do (intuition still playing a part)!

I look ahead and see only the sky before me, below, there is a sheer drop and it is quite a long way down to where a river lies which flows with rapids. So, I got back on my horse, turned around and I rode towards the cavalry, I then stopped again and turned back.

Now It Begins

This time, I galloped full speed ahead and we flew over the edge of the cliff without hesitation. It was such a long way down and I was not sure if we were going to make it. Eventually, we plunged into the water, sunk a little and then came afloat. After which, we were both being pulled along by a gentle current, my horse was on its side, and I thought that she had not made it. I then checked her out to see if she was ok, and she woke from the shock, we both seemed to be fine. The water became shallow and I got up and walked with her through a valley!

There was another vision, that I had during a meditation and once again I was a Native American. It was also very clear and realistic in what I saw. I remember walking through a village, which had been burned down by soldiers. There was no one around, only smoking Tepees that had been set alight.

I was dragging a wooden framed stretcher along with someone laying down on it who had either been injured or was ill. This person was covered over with blankets.

This is all I saw in the vision!

Since I was young, I have always been open to spirituality and yet I questioned my belief in reincarnation for many years until not so long ago. I was always asking myself questions such as; 'What happens after we die'? 'Does the light just go out;

Now It Begins

our body decompose, return to the earth and is that the end?' 'What were we before we came into this life, nothing?' 'If there is life after death what is it like?' 'Do we just sleep wrapped up in a cocoon, then reawaken for the day of judgement and if we are eligible, live for a thousand years of peace on earth, as many Christians believe?'

We all make mistakes in life. It is human nature as we are not perfect. We learn by not repeating those same mistakes over and over again through our own experiences and we can become more aware towards the refinement of ourselves, knowing our true purpose and creating a better place to live on this earth.

So is just one life cycle on earth enough time to totally change our often primitive ways and behavioural patterns within our lives?

Surely, if we returned more than once, we would create a greater awareness.

Perhaps, this is one good reason why we need to go through the cycles of life, death and to be reborn again and most of all, to give us the chance and choice of knowing who we are in the spiritual or physical world.

Admittedly, most of us do not remember our past lives, although I believe all living creatures transmigrate beyond death, as everything continues to exist within cycles in whatever form of energy that may be.

The Soul and Spirit

We may be that tiny little squiggle in the giant Cosmos, but surely we are more than just our bodies, our brains and even our minds?

Many believe humans have souls; of an eternal existence which is said to leave the body and live on after death. Some believe in animism, especially indigenous tribes of people, where the soul also exists in animals, plants, rivers and other natural life habitation. All living things on this earth contain energy and life within, whatever its inner force may be or where it may come from.

There is a separation between the body, soul and spirit, where the soul returns to earth and incarnates eventually into a new born child and the spirit activates the life of the soul, which is a separate entity of its own free will and possibly, continues to exist on the spiritual plane as well as on earth.

It is my belief this is the reason why apparitions and ghosts have been witnessed by many for centuries, because the spirit of the person who has died, remained on earth.

Now It Begins

Are they spirits who have not ascended or crossed over yet, because they had unnatural deaths and have not accepted or perhaps do not even know they have passed on beyond the physical realm, leaving them stranded, lost and trapped in limbo? Or perhaps, they are still seeking revenge here for some injustice that has befallen them, becoming a victim of circumstance whilst they were last here on earth and have not been able to let go.

It is more than likely the trapped spirit would need to accept and let go before the transmigration can finally take place into reincarnation. Just as we live our lives on this earth, we need to accept, take full responsibility for ourselves and then finally, let go of whatever may be necessary before we can move on. As above, is below!

I believe we all have choice even in the spirit world, although for some us, the belief in spirits may be just another waveform of energy!

Reincarnation (Soul Rebirth) With Religions

In most religions, it is believed we will enter an afterlife of some kind and by many, reincarnation or rebirth. In Christianity, reincarnation may have existed until around the 4th century AD. It was then said to have been removed by the Roman Emperor

Now It Begins

Constantine, possibly, through fear of losing control of the church at the time.

There is a difference between reincarnation and rebirth. Most Buddhists believe in rebirth while other religions like Hindus, believe in reincarnation.

Reincarnation can mean; the soul transmigrates into another body after death, leaving a memory which exists of the permanent self.

In Buddhism, or for at least most Buddhists, there is no permanent self which goes beyond death. Yet, there is rebirth; when a person dies the energy does not cease to exist with the body, it is reborn into another form or shape, but without a memory, there is no permanent self. The person who dies is not necessarily the same person as it can transmigrate into another being, an animal or another form of life, much of the transmigration will depend on the Karma of the previous life, from thoughts, words and actions.

In some ways, those lives we may have lived before are no different from the present one which we are living today, as our permanent self (the soul) continues on the journey. We are the result of our past and the karma still carries the burdens and rewards into the present and towards our future, although we may not always know it or remember at the time.

Is this Heaven or Hell?

We are all conditioned to please someone; as a child we want to please our parents, as adults, we may want to please someone else like a boss, or a family member, a wife or husband or perhaps a creator; 'God'. Therefore, when we are admonished for something it can resemble a feeling of what we might perceive to be like being sent to hell. On the contrary, when we are rewarded it can feel like heaven. Of course, it is through our perception of how we think, feel and act about the situation at the time that can make a difference.

We humans, as well as animals are conditioned and programmed to respond to being rewarded and chastised through our deeds. So, on a greater level of understanding, could we already be living a continuous cycle of heaven and hell, one which we may have experienced many times before and are still experiencing today?

Many will perceive their lives and the world they live in as a promising heavenly abode and others will see much of their lives as a living hell!

To a great extent, we are the masters of our own destiny and we create our own heaven and hell!

Everything is as it is. It is Our Perception That Really Matters!

This gives us all a greater understanding of the reasons why past lives may exist, and to possibly know why we have chosen to come down on earth again to be reborn into the cycle of reincarnation.

Now It Begins

Another reason for this might be that there is a karmic debt which is necessary to be paid off to someone, or to society, or it may be that you may have some unfinished business with others which you left behind in your previous life and that you may wish to change or to put right.

We are all passing through life so quickly like a breeze, yet we all make our marks that become imprinted in the soul and incarnates until the cycles are complete. After which, it may then be a time for judgment for us humans. Until that day, we will continue to learn, to suffer and to give and receive joy.

Child Awareness of Reincarnation

Many children from different parts of the world have recalled and remembered their past lives, often without being aware of what is actually happening, as it comes so naturally to them. I have heard parents saying that their daughter said as they were driving along: 'I used to live over there before, but you were not my mummy then.' Another child in Scotland said 'I used to live over there with my boys.' Often children are aware of another existence from around the age of three and up until around six years old.

The seven year cycle takes effect as we progress into adulthood creating a greater awareness in the conscious mind, bringing forth changes and re-

Now It Begins

learning to cope with the problems of modern day life. In the meantime, the unconscious mind is not lost but may remain in the background except when one has a strong and vivid imagination. Otherwise, remembering our past lives is usually accessed through our dreams and visions, the feelings of déjà vu, which are more common, meditation and, of course, through past life regression therapy.

There is so much evidence in the world these days that can be found on the internet and from other sources, where incredible stories of children and adults have been recorded or witnessed by many who have experienced past lives.

There have also been many recorded cases from the clients of psychiatrists and regressionists where evidence of past lives has been found, when researched.

Past Life Regression

In my work as a hypnotherapist, I have given past life regression to a number of people. Some in their past lives were wealthy and some were poor but there were few that I have given regression to who have been so famous, believing, for example; they were seeing themselves as Cleopatra or other very famous characters.

It is more probable the person in question would be seeing the queen, possibly from a distance, rather than being her, but of course, someone has to be her and I have not met her yet!

Those to whom I have given past life regression have been mainly women who all responded very well in a genuine manner as I guided them on an exciting journey through their unknown past. Most of these clients were very down to earth and responsible people, and some had no idea what to expect whilst under hypnosis.

During the session I always write an account of what has taken place, their whereabouts and who they might have been in a past life.

Most will experience an average of around three past lives depending on their ability to visualise and the time permitting. Each life can be very different from another. This is one important reason why we may return to this present life, so we may learn! Just as our DNA is the carrier of genetic information, we are the strengths and the weaknesses of our ancestors.

One lady to whom I gave past life regression had a problem with her husband in this life. She was with him for many years and was the motivator in the marriage, although because of this, the marriage was becoming a struggle, yet she was still trying her best to support her relationship. Under regression, the lady experienced four previous lives, although one of them was a child and went no further as she was lost, yet it was still significant. The other three lives were people of different eras, but strangely enough, each one had the same problem of having difficulties with their husbands, three in total and most of the time they were not visible in any of the past lives. It was quite amazing, as the client experienced each previous life her voice changed, and she was also expressing her emotions, like crying. When she experienced life as a child she sounded like one. This was not the sort of person to act this way.

The journey into past lives with regression can be an exciting one, although if there is an issue that has not been dealt with in the past, it will often present itself in the present. I take clients into the inter-life while moving from one past life to the next.

The Interlife

After we have passed on from a life cycle on earth and before we incarnate to the next one, we enter the 'Interlife,' this is a place between lives. It is where we can look at our previous life and reflect; to ask for forgiveness, or to forgive those who are either there with us on a spiritual plane or those who we left behind on earth.

It is a place of peace and serenity, calmness and tranquillity and where the soul is cleansed. It is a place to learn and grow spiritually before we move on into the next or present life. On a level of a far greater depth and capacity, infinitely, we are all one

Now It Begins

with the Universe and its energy. Everything exists within cycles, all is recycled.

Karma

Karma is an ancient Indian Sanskrit word which means 'action'. Karma responds to whatever your actions are with a reaction, even it is not an immediate one.

The most important thing to remember here is not to blame something or someone else for what might be of our own making; through our thoughts, words or actions. When we do this, it will only create more misfortune by hurting ourselves or another, and will also bring negative Karma upon ourselves. Be responsible for your own actions, by doing good deeds to others, this will also create good Karma!

We reap what we sow; this is the law of cause and effect.

Phase Nine

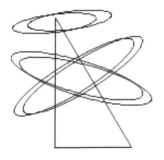

Now Is The Only Time

Phase Nine

Now Is The Only Time

Live Your Life as You Really Mean It

Make use of everything you have experienced from your past and what you may have learned from it. If it is a negative experience, turn it around to your advantage and make it positive in your life. If it is a positive one, enhance it and let it manifest and grow. Everything is there to teach us something. We all have so little time on this earth, even though some

Now It Begins

moments may seem to pass slowly when we are anguished, in pain or even when you are not making full use of your life and have become bored.

There is so much for us all to do out there, and at times we seem to go so fast, as if there is not enough time to do the things that need to be done. Make the most of your life, as every minute is so precious.

Now is the Only Time you Own

It does surprise me at times, when we all know we are taking nothing with us in the material way when we leave this planet, yet some of us hold on for dear life to our possessions. It is true we all form attachments to certain things in life and sometimes it is hard to let go of them, although many of us do become stuck.

Throughout this book, I have talked about letting go. I have said nothing is permanent in life and to everything there is a purpose. We have all been conditioned to believe that by serving the illusion to suit ourselves and not the reality of helping one another in the world; it will give us greater satisfaction in achieving. This is not so; the key to our future lies in working together.

'What does it profit a man to gain the world and to lose his Soul'!

Now It Begins

Story: The Old Man Who had Everything and the Angel of Death

When the angel of death appeared to the old man who had everything, he said; "Your time has come!"

The old man replied; "Please just give me one more month to accomplish the things that I haven't done yet, I need more time"

"You have had your life on this earth and now it is time for you to leave."

"OK, just give me one more week; I will give anything you may ask of me. I have great wealth" the old man begged.

The angel of death replied, "You now have nothing to offer that is of any use."

"One more hour, surely you can give this, just a little time? That's not asking too much, is it?" Throughout his life, the old man had always bargained and was used to getting his own way with people who had less than him. The angel of death spoke for the last time

"Throughout your whole life you have given little to others and when you have done you always expected or demanded something in return, instead of giving from your heart and then walking away. You have also taken a lot more from others than they would have willingly given to you, and have always said to

Now It Begins

them everything has its price, and nobody said life was fair! It has not been fair, because you have taken too much and contributed little. Even if I had given you more time, you would not be satisfied, because you always want more. It is now time for you to accept and finally let go."

With all his wealth and riches, the old man could not buy one more second of his life. His time had come.

Accepting the Journey into the Unknown

It is a great thing to have a clear conscience before we depart from this earth. Of course, we have all made mistakes and errors within our lives, which has often left us feeling guilt and remorse for ourselves and others, but, this is now a time to forgive. As Oscar Wilde said 'Every saint has a past and every sinner has a future.'

No matter what age we may be; if we can learn to be open to accepting the journey into the unknown when we finally depart from this life, we will become greater beings and free ourselves from our conditioning. In the western world, most of us have not been taught or shown how to deal with facing death. In the East however, this has been quite the opposite with religious and spiritual beliefs.

I once witnessed a funeral in Bali, Indonesia, with over one hundred musicians and singers. The body, which was inside a papier-mâché life size horse, was then removed and cremated. This seems to be a joyful occasion as in many other countries of the world. The person who had passed on, his spirit was set free, (providing he was willing to let go of this world of course).

Spirituality in the Holy City of Benares (Varanasi)

Varanasi (Benares) India is a very spiritual holy city and possibly one of the oldest if not, the oldest living city in the world where many Hindus, Jains and even Buddhists visit for important rituals and to prepare for the afterlife. It is also a place where many are cremated and their ashes are scattered in the sacred Ganges River.

In Varanasi the energy is amazing; people come to visit from all over the world. It has been a sacred city for at least three thousand years and still thrives today. In the day time, there are many 'Pyres', funerals which take place beside the River Ganges. There are platforms where piles of wood are stacked for the cremations and the bodies are laid on them, usually wrapped in white cloth.

During the evenings at sunset in Varanasi, everyone gathers around for 'Puja' a religious Hindu ceremony of offerings, where there is singing and chanting. There are priests with lamps of incense and oil who

Now It Begins

stand on the platforms and swing their lamps back and forth. The atmosphere is spiritual and uplifting.

For those, who are old and poor and cannot afford the wood for their own funeral, which is a special wood gathered for burning, they will stay in a tower which lies close by the cremation platforms. There, they will ask for money from people until they have enough for the wood and their funeral. It is an honour for Hindus to be cremated by the sacred river Ganges.

I witnessed one cremation when I was in Nepal some years ago; it was a woman who looked as though she would have been in her thirties. The lady was wrapped in a white shroud, and some men who were standing around her placed a yellow cloth over the body. The face was showing and the men placed small flowers individually over her body, they then placed a coin in her mouth, (possibly for good luck or to pay for the travelling expenses into the afterlife) and proceeded to paint her face and the shroud with red dye. After doing this, they walked around her about nine times and sprinkled a flammable liquid over her and then set the body alight. She had a very peaceful expression on her face, without tension.

Most of us on this earth have no wish to die, but, if we can learn to accept and let go of fears of the unknown it will allow the transition to become easier for when the time will come.

Now It Begins

There is no end; it is only one door closing and another opening, taking us on an unknown journey into a new beginning.

Phase Ten

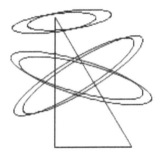

The Higher Self

Phase Ten

The Higher Self

Tuning into the Higher Self

Each person's realisation is different from another's; the key is to find your own.

Through our higher self, we create understanding and through our lower self we are experiencing what we may need to learn.

Who are we? What we are not; is just our brain and body. We are much more. We control the brain and body through our minds. Although the mind is a very powerful tool, in fact, we are more than our minds; we are one with the cosmic energy, which is infinite.

We have all the resources that we need to achieve and create, the answer lies within each of us.

When you are confused about certain issues, just go into the quietness of your mind, find a place to relax and be still. After five minutes or so; ask for an answer to the problem that is bothering you. The more you are aligned and in tune with yourself, the faster you will receive an answer to your problem. This may take a little practise at first, but after a while the answers will flow, because you are tuning into your higher self, to your unconscious mind or to your spiritual guides. Wherever it might be coming from, do not be afraid. Just relax, allow it to come and accept and you will be amazed at what you receive. Our unconscious mind is like a video recorder holding all memories of our life cycle, from birth to the time we depart from this earth and beyond. The only way we can access our unconscious mind to receive the answers we seek is to be totally relaxed and to allow any thoughts that emerge to pass.

Accept the answers to your question. Always only ask one question at a time, otherwise you will flood and create confusion, also be specific and precise in whatever it is you are asking. If you are not clear about what you want, it will return in the same way, scrambled and confused. This is the same as when you ask the universe for something, it will always return in the same way.

The Three Levels (Physical, Mental and Spiritual)

The material plane vibrates on a slower and lower level of energy than that of a higher plane, which resonates at a much faster frequency.

If we could separate energy, it might be said three main forms of energy exist, on earth, the sky and heavenly bodies.

As in humanity; there is the average person who goes about their everyday work without thinking too much, just getting on with what they need to be doing.

Now It Begins

Secondly; there is the intellectual person who uses his or her mind to a great extent, working out and planning everything that needs to be done in the present and in the future. Just like the average person, they are both seeking joy and happiness externally to themselves on the material level, seeking and striving for worldly possessions.

Then, there is the one who allows things to happen naturally, because they already know what needs to be done before it happens. Through meditation and connecting with the higher self or soul, this person finds inner peace and maintains their presence in the present time, the now.

Yet, a person who is uneducated and lives a very simple life can sometimes have so much more wisdom than one who has studied intellectually all their life.

Just as a child can often surprise so many with their wisdom through their openness and innocence, this kind of knowledge is eternal and goes far beyond the levels of education and intellect.

The ego can often take control of one, creating a blockage, restricting the flow from progressing in a spiritual direction towards understanding and accepting ourselves from within and others externally.

No matter, if you have an understanding on a physical, mental or spiritual level, we all have a purpose on this earth to bring forth change, by

Now ItBegins

helping one another and this is now needed more than ever.

Whatever level of spirituality you may attain, no one can be completely in the physical, just as no one can be totally spiritual, as long as we remain in our given physical bodies, and as long as we are here on this earth, the body, mind and spirit all work together. Some of us will continue to work on a lower level of vibration and others will continue to work on a higher frequency, we each have our purpose.

Although the one who develops through their higher self will eventually become more detached and almost asleep, distant from the material plane and issues of the world and from their higher self and spirituality.

Just as the person who takes full part in playing the games and serving the illusion of this world, they will also become more detached and may regress from their higher self and spirituality, remaining asleep.

With these changes that are beginning to take place in this world and within our lives, it is now time to awaken and move away from fear and draw unconditional love towards us, as well as sending it out and accepting a higher source of energy does exist, which also comes from within, as above.

More than ever before, we are now being given an opportunity to be open towards receiving this channelled energy, raising our levels of vibration to a higher state of consciousness and being ready for the great changes in this world that are now occurring. This opportunity allows us to rise beyond the fears which will not only continue to exist amongst many, but will also spread amongst the world causing greater confusion and catastrophes.

Nothing goes unrewarded; if our lower self is open and willing towards raising the vibrations from within, we will also be helped from the higher source, meeting us somewhere in between. Once we see what we have been given, we will understand more of the reality, our true selves, of knowing who we are and what really matters in life. We will also come to understand global fear is part of the illusion which we will overcome.

We have the choice to ignore the signs being shown to us or to change, as it is now time to shift and raise our levels of vibration.

Our internal power lies within and all truth is known and understood. External power exists outside ourselves, trying to control and searching for the answers in the world we live in.

Raising your Levels of Vibration

It is important and necessary to raise our levels of consciousness, if we want to find peace, harmony and beauty. All of this can only be attained from within.

First, we must be aware of our thoughts and feelings and to know who we really are. We can do this by opening our hearts and surrendering, by letting go of

Now It Begins

those negative thoughts, fears and limitations that we have held on to for so long.

Your soul knows who you are, only you have forgotten, by being in touch with our inner selves we can know who we are; you just have to be honest with yourself.

When you raise your vibration, you are raising your levels of the conscious and unconscious mind and are attuning to a higher frequency; this is the beginning of the process towards changing our lives. At whichever level your awareness may lie; by remaining in the present time, thinking positive thoughts for yourself and others, enjoying your life and allowing yourself to feel good, is the key towards the development of your higher self.

When we are not enjoying, or not feeling good about ourselves, when we are thinking negative thought patterns and possibly becoming angry, we are then vibrating on a lower frequency level. This not only blocks our energy but will eventually become sluggish and restrict the flow towards receiving from the universe. On this lower level of vibration, we attract doubt and confusion.

When a person has a positive thought around 100 people can pick up the energy surrounding him or her.

This is the same as the world in its present stage as we move towards the new vibrational shift raising our levels of consciousness to a higher frequency of awareness and understanding.

It is our true power which comes through our higher self from the universe. Our internal power is everlasting and eternal. There are many ways of raising our vibration; for example:

Yoga

Its name is derived from a Sanskrit word 'Yuj' which means 'to yoke' or to 'unite'. Originating in India, yoga has been practised for thousands of years and is taken very seriously in the eastern part of the world. Those who are dedicated to its practise incorporate the body, mind and spirit. This is the unity connecting the physical, mental and higher self of realisation and oneness.

In the West yoga is mainly used for exercise, although many are now adopting pranayama which is breath control, combined with meditation. Yoga can increase flexibility, lubricating the joints and muscles. It decreases anxiety and depression, reduces high blood pressure, giving a feeling of well being and inner peace and truly raising our vibrations.

Natural foods

These days there are few totally natural foods which when eaten in excess can sometimes be harmful. However, a healthy food intake maintains a healthy state of mind and body. Know what works for you;

Now ItBegins

find the balance in your life by not eating too much or too little. Change any unhealthy eating habits.

Find out what is good for you; fresh fruits and vegetables, oily fish, anything which supplies good nutrition. You will certainly notice changes, feel a lighter energy which is vibrating on a higher frequency. This is a certain way to raise your level of vibration and to feeling good.

Water

Drinking plenty of water is also very important. If you wait until you are thirsty before drinking you are almost definitely dehydrated already. Most of the tissues and organs of the body are made up of two thirds water and need to be topped up regularly. Drinking water detoxifies the body, replenishes and sends oxygen to every cell. Water regulates the temperature of the body and cools the brain allowing it to function well, which prevents tiredness and headaches. Being well hydrated is very good for the skin and acts as a lubricant for our joints. Ditch the fizzy drink and take a cool, refreshing glass of water. Be hydrated, behealthy.

Exercising

Even though we can become a little lazy or it is hard to find the time to exercise we all realise how beneficial it is towards keeping us healthy. It raises our level of vibration and helps us to live longer. You will sleep better and wake up feeling recharged and

Now It Begins

alert. It aids weight control, increasing the metabolism, rejuvenating the body's cells and lifting moods to give more physical and mental energy. Exercise can reduce the risk of heart disease, strokes and other illnesses improving your mental health and greater sense of well being.

Being around Nature

What better way to feel good about yourself than to be surrounded by nature. Being around nature increases your mental well being and spiritual development. It can reduce stress, healing us through its energy and allowing us to focus, in a relaxed way, on the purpose and meaning of our lives. Nature can reduce and lift us from depression. Exchange your concrete enclosure for a walk in the park and feel nature's energy empower you.

Laughter

Laughter is especially a healer within itself, it increases the oxygen in the blood cells, strengthens the immune system to help fight off the antigens within our bodies and greatly reduces stress.

The more you become aligned with yourself, the more you will raise your energy of vibrations.

Now It Begins

Meditation

The higher self is our soul or higher soul; we are the
soul, as we are more than just our physical bodies,
our thoughts and mind.

Now It Begins

Through meditation we can experience the higher self, the higher soul.

There is no separation, as we are one. Our physical body on the lower self is a vehicle to enable us to do what we need to be able to do and take us where we need to go whilst here on earth. Our thoughts and emotions control the body, just as the mind may watch over our thoughts and emotions, beyond is the soul and everything works together as one.

The more we attune and align ourselves with the higher self, the more focused we become in raising the vibration.

In the progression of connecting with the higher soul, it will be necessary at different stages to let go and free yourself from any restrictions and limitations you may have acquired and taken on in the past or, anything which may be blocking your path towards spiritual development and enlightenment. One is not expected to give up everything overnight, as this can have repercussions in making the journey too difficult but, as we become more aware of the body mind and spirit, we will find it becomes easer to release that which no longer serves a purpose.

On a higher level; the body is a temple and it serves no purpose blocking our spiritual pathway by abusing our bodies with toxic harmful substances or foods. These foods and substances can have a detrimental effect later on in life, just as negative thoughts and words can pollute the body. More often than not; it is the negative impressions of the mind which will create more diseases. As the body is a temple, it should be given respect if we are to reach the higher self.

When we stray too many times from the path we become disconnected from our higher self, the soul and soul purpose. We may even forget why we started the journey in the first place.

The higher self or soul eventually leads us to the path of enlightenment, to know God through the self, as we are one. Just as we are connected to a higher source, our spirit guides, angels and higher beings are connecting with us, creating an open channel.

We can remember who we are and know our true soul purpose. One way to do this is through meditation.

Meditation is a state of being, remaining in the present.

By allowing your mind to drift and relax, you will become more aware of your inner and higher self. The more you become relaxed, the more you will find stillness and know your true inner self and the more you practise meditation, the easier it will become to clear your mind and to focus on the state of being.

The main purpose of meditation is to clear the mind from wandering and to clear the mind of the thoughts which have built up throughout the day or throughout your life.

Now It Begins

Concentration on the void, space and emptiness is necessary when focusing with the mind. Creating awareness is also an essential part of meditation; this can be done through breathing and chanting sounds like; 'Om' or 'Aum'. The eyes may either remain open or closed. When open; one can focus on an object by placing a candle or a crystal in front at a short distance. When using a candle, please take care it is in a safe place when alight and can do no harm in the surrounding area or to anyone. Otherwise, close the eyes, some find meditation easer in this way. With eyes closed, you can focus on the third eye (in between both eyes); the name for this in Sanskrit is 'Ajna' and is also the connection to the pituitary and pineal glands which are linked to psychic awareness.

However, if the eyes are closed; take care not to fall asleep. When this happens it can be a resistance of some kind, a blockage which may exist from your past and is restricting the flow by stopping you from meditating.

This can be very common, especially when first attempting to meditate, as many thoughts can rush through from the unconscious to the conscious part of the mind. Some may cause confusion and even create uncomfortable feelings; such as anger or sadness.

At this stage, many people give up and say they have tried to meditate but cannot. This is where patience is required to overcome the distractions.

Now It Begins

If this happens it is ok, do not be concerned, as it is a necessary process for clearing the blockages, which have built up over the years, freeing you from the restrictions and worries of your past. Remember; the greatest fear; is fear itself.

Allow this to happen naturally and work with it; let all of those thoughts just flow through and do not try to hold on to any of them, because they have no importance, or power over you and serve no purpose while you are meditating. As you continue to meditate it will become easer every time, allowing you to focus on the inner self.

Of course, even for some of those who have been meditating many years, they may still occasionally experience at times all kinds of thoughts which may appear during meditation. As we become more aware of our lower and higher selves, we will know what is true when those thoughts present themselves at the time of meditation and we will also know if a certain issue needs to be dealt with or ignored.

As I have mentioned before, this is also because; when an issue from our past has not been dealt with, it will often be repeated and can show up in many ways, letting us know either something is wrong or there is some unfinished business that may still exist. Occurring also in dreams as well as in meditation, once again, it is the monster which shrinks or disappears in the nightmare when we face our fears.

Now It Begins

Breathing in the correct way is very important, as this can help physically, mentally and spiritually. When one chants the sound of 'Om'; it resonates and connects with the third eye enhancing our awareness and vibration of the higher self.

At the first stage when meditating; one should inhale and exhale through the nose, taking deep and slow breaths from the stomach area only and not the chest.

If you are not sure how to do this; take the left hand, place it on the chest area and the right hand below on your stomach and then breathe in and out. Only the right hand should move. When inhaling the stomach goes out and when exhaling the stomach goes back in. Relax the breathing when it no longer becomes the focal point anymore but continues in the background with a steady and easy flow. Once you have done this, you can expand your awareness. Be aware of the silence surrounding you (making sure there is silence), before, after and in between the breaths or chants, allowing peace, harmony and tranquillity to exist.

Inner calmness and stillness are the first stages of meditation before reaching one's higher self. As we progress with meditation our mind becomes still and the chattering stops, the stress of every day life fades into the background and no longer has or holds any power over us.

Now ItBegins

When we experience our higher self, or the higher soul we can experience joy, happiness and unconditional love as well as the connection with the higher beings, spirit guides and angels.

One should never actually 'try' to achieve the goal of reaching the higher self during meditation as it is a natural and gradual process which will take much time; for some, many years, just as one would not expect to climb Mount Everest without training.

There are no short cuts. For those who have used certain substances to attain the higher self; they may certainly experience euphoria and other altered states, although this will only exist as a temporary state. After the effects have worn off, it will not only bring the person back down to earth, experiencing their lower self and often in a negative way with confused emotions but, they may regress, finding it so much more difficult to meditate in the future, which will be just like starting over again from the beginning.

In another way, when a person claims to have achieved and reached a certain higher level in meditation, they are possibly only trying to impress others by promoting and fulfilling their ego, which will eventually block their path from progressing any further in the future with meditation.

Now It Begins

At first, when meditating, many thoughts will enter into your mind. Just allow them to pass, do not try to control them. The purpose is to focus on the now, in the state of being. If at any time a particular thought reoccurs after each meditation acknowledge what it is, as it is more than likely, showing you something that needs to be dealt with and then released.

In the beginning; practise meditation for around ten minutes in the morning or evening, or both. When you feel ready, you can increase the length of time to say; twenty minutes, then to thirty minutes and so on. Just do whatever you can. Doing some meditation is always better than none.

When you are meditating at home, find a comfortable chair to sit on with your feet firmly on the ground, legs and arms uncrossed and palms facing upwards by either placing them on your lap or beside you. If you wish, you can connect the first finger with your thumb of each hand. If you prefer, sit on the floor with the legs crossed, and if you are used to yoga you can place yourself in a half or full Lotus position. Whether you sit on a chair or on the floor, it will be necessary to keep the head and back straight in alignment, so your breathing is not restricted, allowing the energy to flow throughout the body.

Just allowing yourself to relax as you focus on the void, not trying to control any thoughts, but letting them pass through and becoming detached, merely to observe those thoughts as they gradually disappear, and as you do this with practise you become more and more focused, calm and aligned with yourself. After your meditation; return to the state of consciousness, feeling your physical body by moving your fingers, your toes and other areas; also becoming aware of your surroundings.

Then take a nice deep breath in and out, and feel good about yourself, refreshing and replenishing your whole body. When you feel ready, slowly open your eyes and come back to full waking consciousness. Give thanks to the universe for your meditation and for all things.

Now ground yourself. The easiest way to do this is to take some deep breaths in and out and imagine you are being pulled down into the earth. You are being grounded.

If you are sitting on a chair, you can imagine; like tree roots going deep into the ground which are attached and wrapped around your feet as you are being pulled down into the earth, making a connection with the mother earth.

Build meditation into a part of your everyday life, until it becomes hard to imagine living without it.

Visualisation

Visualisation also plays an important part in meditation and with the laws of the universe. By using our imagination 'we create all that exists around us'.

Now ItBegins

Just as with meditation; many people say they cannot visualise, this is only because they have created a block to belief.

We all use our imagination in many ways throughout the day, which is the same as visualisation. Our imagination is much stronger than willpower, as I have explained before; regarding when one wants to give up a habit like smoking or eating chocolates; the imagination often wins most times, as the 'will', may battle against it and give up.

When we change our thought patterns using the imagination in a positive way, then we can succeed in what we are trying to achieve. Quite often when you say; 'try not to', or 'don't' imagine something, you will more than likely imagine it, because you are giving the unconscious mind a command which will respond to the word; 'don't'. It receives this message and understands it as a positive one; 'do'. This is why children do the opposite when you say; 'don't' to them. Children are also excellent at using their imagination.

So, the imagination can be a powerful tool.

When we use our imagination in a positive way, many things can be achieved, just as one may imagine seeing oneself being healed from an illness, this can often have a very strong and beneficial effect, because the mind takes care of the body.

The more you practise the art of visualisation, the easier it will become. Through the images of our

Now It Begins

mind's eye, we can create the world we want to live in.

Use visualisation as a tool during or after meditating, by bringing the things in life you truly want closer towards you.

See it, hear it, feel it and believe it is happening.

Energy Centres Within and Beyond the Physical Body: Auras

An aura is an energy field that melds with and radiates out beyond the physical body.

Everything that exists is made up of energy, atoms, subatomic particles etc, and we are all part of this vibrational energy. Auras do not only exist around living objects, but around non-living objects as well.

The aura surrounding a person can show if one is angry or calm, developed on a spiritual level, or if one is suffering from an illness. Of course, not everyone has the ability to see this form of energy, but we most certainly are able to see the auras of ourselves or of others to some degree.

For those who are highly spiritually advanced, they will have strong auras showing a colour of yellow above their head.

The majority of people on earth have weak auras, which may show as dull, this is because they may have had so much negativity in their lives with so much anger and jealousy or even hatred and have not been able to let go of these trapped emotions. Just as their whole persona can also give an appearance of some kind of heaviness when one is sufficiently aware to see this in another. Although we are all capable of change which will cleanse the aura, until that time the energy surrounding them will continue to be dull.

Children also have the ability to see the auras of others before they reach the age of seven. They may even become frightened when they look up and gaze above an adults head (as they often do) and notice the colour is dull or dark, as this can often be a reflection of the adults characteristics. They could also be happy and smiling when they see an aura of someone that is light or brightly coloured. This is perhaps one reason why babies cry or are happy when they see a stranger. As we all know; children are perceptive and can be very honest, they also have a clear aura because of their innocence.

For thousands of years people have seen auras, more so in the past than in these modern times. Although with technology and special equipment being used, it can now reveal the auras and colours within the inner and outer bodies.

In times past, paintings of religious, spiritually advanced people like Jesus, Buddha and other saints were depicted with golden or white halos above and around their heads. This symbolises not only their

Now ItBegins

spiritual awareness, but the energy which surrounded them.

We all have the capability to see auras. If you do not believe it exists, then you probably will never see an aura, although many of you will have already seen auras and may not have even noticed.

An aura can often be seen around the body in a reasonably short period of time especially, if one trains in the correct way. One way to do this is to stand relaxed in front of a mirror at a distance of around five or six feet. Now begin to stare at your forehead, just above between the eyes, this is where the third eye is situated. Keep the lighting generally soft and stand with a reasonably plain and not too brightly coloured wall in the background behind you.

Concentrate on this area for ten to fifteen minutes, if at first; it becomes too tiring to focus, cut down the length of time to thirty seconds and then spend more time as you progress. After doing this; relax and check your image through the mirror, the area surrounding your head, if you like; around your body as well (although it is probably better to do this gradually). After a period of time you may start to see a haze surrounding your head and body as you develop. Some may even see certain colours appear in the haze, which can also have meaning; an indication of your health and spiritual development.

Give yourself some time each day to become familiar with the energy surrounding your body. It can be

Now It Begins

quite an exciting discovery when it first appears. There are no set rules as to how long one needs before seeing their own aura, although it should be given at least ten days or more when focusing, before expecting any results. As I have said, some will develop sooner than others.

The Chakras

There is no separation between the chakras and auras as they interact as one unit. The chakras communicate from within the physical body through to the outer subtle bodies of the auric field and vice versa.

There are seven major energy centres of the body that have been known to exist for thousands of years by yogis and other enlightened masters mainly from the East. They have not been recognised in the western field of medicine in the past and neither will they be found in an autopsy. These sacred energy centres are known as; 'Chakras', which comes from the ancient classical Indian name in Sanskrit meaning; 'wheel' or 'disk'. Each of the chakras is connected with one of the seven endocrine glands of the body and correlate to major nerve ganglia branching out from the spinal column. There are also hundreds or possibly thousands of minor Chakras which exist and run along the meridian channels within the body that are recognised and understood by those who practise acupuncture.

Now It Begins

The Chakras begin at the base of the spine and continue to move upwards towards the top and above the head; each chakra has an effect on the area of the body it surrounds, physically, emotionally, mentally and spiritually.

It has been said; each chakra spins and vibrates at a high frequency or at least, when we are in good health. If an illness should occur, the chakras may slow down, stop and even continue to rotate in a reverse order from clockwise to anti clockwise or vice versa. Each chakra should be equally balanced with the other one for a natural flow to occur within the body.

Chakras are usually only seen by certain masters who have practised the art of meditation for several years and have developed their spirituality to a high degree by training in this way. However, there are some who are also highly developed clairvoyantly or spiritually who may see these energy centres within the body.

As with most things that exist within our lives; there is a positive and a negative side, this is the same for each chakra. If a chakra is out of balance it will in turn affect the one next to it.

The Root Chakra (Muladhara, colour: red) is located at the base of the spine, this chakra relates to our foundation, survival, stability in life, and connection to the earth; this is our lower self. It is also associated

Now ItBegins

with our physical nature, the circulation of blood, bones and muscles. When this chakra is functioning correctly and balanced, it can give us vitality, physical energy, health, prosperity and security.

However; if the root chakra is open too wide, it may be a person, so to speak, who enjoys living in the flesh i.e. excessive eating of red meat, drinking alcohol, sexual pleasures, gambling etc. This can create physical problems of the body in the area which is related to this chakra. The root chakra is also associated with illusion, anger and greed.

Creating a balance for the first chakra (grounding): Treat your body as a temple keeping reasonably physically fit with exercise and eating a balanced diet. Avoid alcohol or, at least, use in moderation. Detach a little from worldly pleasures and learn the art of relaxation or meditation to create calmness within.

The second chakra (Swadhisthana) (colour: orange) is located in the abdominal area and is related to our physical well being, emotions and our feelings. This is the seat of our emotions and where we store them. The sacral chakra also represents self respect, our self worth and respecting others, giving us independence and joy. The negative aspects are: withdrawn, envy and jealousy, guilt, blame, resentment.

Creating a balance for the second chakra (letting go): Give yourself the love you deserve, being in

Now It Begins

touch with the inner child, letting go of all the hurts; negativity, resentment, emotional feelings and anger which has blocked and restricted you in your past from moving on into the present, accepting change and feeling good about yourself.

The third chakra (Manipura) (colour: yellow) is located in the solar plexus, it is related to confidence, intellect, our ego and optimism. This is the power centre of the self; it is where the chi energy or life force is stored, giving the ability to achieve.

The negative aspects of this chakra are; pride, vanity, self righteousness, external power in controlling the self and others, egoism, fear and worries

Creating a balance for the third chakra (knowing): To go beyond the ego, knowing yourself and understanding others, achieving without effort, acceptance of yourself, awareness.

The fourth chakra (Anahata) (colours: green, pink) is located in the area of the heart and is related to healing, unconditional love, sharing, giving, compassion, openness and peace. This chakra integrates with the mind and body, going beyond the ego.

The negative aspects of this chakra are avarice, selfishness, meanness, miserly tendencies, hatred, vulnerability, conditional love.

Creating a balance for the fourth chakra (unconditional love): be open, and when giving, give

Now It Begins

from your heart to others unconditionally with compassion, sharing and networking. Practise meditation with the openness of the heart chakra, giving unconditional love for all on this planet, being honest.

The fifth chakra (Vishuddha) (colours: turquoise, sky blue) is located in the throat and related to communication, self expression, sounds and vibration.

The negative aspects of this chakra are quietness, timidity, shyness, difficulty in expressing, arrogance, self righteousness, aggressiveness, violence.

Creating a balance for the fifth chakra (clarity): being who you truly are, speaking with an open mind and with clarity, singing and chanting to unblock throat chakra.

The sixth chakra (Ajna) (colours: indigo, blue) is located in the third eye, related to; awareness, psychic powers, clairvoyance, the higher self, telepathy, visualisation, spirit, the all; 'Seeing Eye'. Jesus said; 'The light of the body is the eye; therefore when your eye is single, the whole body is filled with light, but when the eye is evil, the whole body also is filled with darkness'.

The negative aspects of this chakra are egoism, pride, manipulation and lack of vision.

Creating a balance for the sixth chakra (seeing from within): having clear vision, creating an

Now ItBegins

awareness, using intuition and acceptance of the higher self.

The seventh chakra (Sahasrara) (colours: Violet, gold, white) is located in the crown and is related to enlightenment, beyond the physical, spiritual, understanding, and an all knowing, detachment. The negative aspects of this chakra are being withdrawn, not grounded and not connecting to spirit.

Creating a balance for the seventh chakra (oneness): being an open channel, connecting to spirit, at peace with one's higher self and spirituality, connecting with the universe, meditation with the crown chakra. Remember to ground afterwards.

Other chakras are said to exist beyond the physical, and the twelfth chakra is most highly spiritual. This chakra has been witnessed by some in the past; as seeing a golden or sometimes white halo above the heads of those who are enlightened. It has also been noticed; around the crown area, a golden lotus flower.

People of many religions have been known to wear decorative golden, yellow and white hats in the past and up to this present day, representing the higher self. This can also be seen symbolically, with royalty hence; the golden crown they wear above the heads, often padded with purple or violet, which is the colour of the crown chakra (a poor reflection of the true higher self). Many holy buildings around the world also have gold domes or a golden ball at the top, these all represent the highest chakra.

Now It Begins

With yoga becoming so popular these days in the western part of the world, more people are now slowly becoming aware of chakras, even though they may not know what they mean. The veil has finally lifted; and many of us are now experiencing a greater awareness within ourselves and of others, also expanding the capacity of our minds and brains. We are now becoming more open to a higher vibration which has been given by our spirit guides or others of the source.

This will give us the ability to tune into higher frequencies and eventually know and be able to see these energy centres do exist, as they are all a part of us and we are a part of the oneness.

If we could compare the world to where it might be positioned in the way of looking at chakras and energy; I would say it may lie within the third chakra! Meaning we are still caught up with ego, external power and the need for controlling others. This is a major reason why there are wars; poverty and famine and until we learn to let go, it will still continue to exist.

With the shift that is happening, we will eventually move on, though not for all, but for many it will free us from being stuck in the past and give us a clearer pathway to move into the heart chakra. Hopefully, the rest of the world will follow before it is too late.

Now It Begins

The Kundalini

Kundalini is also a Sanskrit word and means; 'coiled'. There is a latent energy which lies within us all and it is called the; 'Kundalini'. Yogis and other Masters of the past have realised a life force has existed within the physical body since ancient times and for most of us; this energy lies dormant and coiled up within the base chakra of the spine. The Kundalini was often represented as a 'Cobra', which sat on the crowns of ancient Egyptian Pharaohs and also sat with or on top of the head of 'Shiva' the ancient Hindu god. The Kundalini has also been known as the sleeping serpent or the serpent fire, in fact; it could be likened as two serpents. You may have noticed the symbol that is associated with the medical profession, the 'Caduceus' with the two serpents entwining around a staff and at the top is a pair of wings. The wings are the crown chakra. When the Kundalini energy is awakened it coils around and activates each chakra three and a half times crossing over from the left to the right side and rising upwards to the crown and returning back down to the base chakra where it begins symbolising a figure eight. This energy also rises through the centre of the spinal column, which is a hollow type canal called; the Sushumna'. There are two channels of energy; the left is called; 'Ida' and the right 'Pingala'. These are also related to the left and right hemispheres of the brain. The left being masculine which controls the right side of the body and the right is feminine which controls the left side

Now It Begins

of the body.

The Kundalini can be awakened in different ways, sometimes involuntarily or voluntarily with the correct training. When it has been activated in an unknowledgeable way, it may create psychological or physical problems within the mind and body. This can happen through accidents, bereavements, shocks and in other ways like; taking certain drugs, especially psychedelic ones, which may awaken the Kundalini but not in a steady and slow, progressive way. Instead, it may send the energy rushing through the chakras and nervous system, reaching the crown chakra and possibly not returning.

When this happens; it can leave the person totally ungrounded and confused, unable to communicate with others and feeling disoriented and even paranoid. For those who are generally reasonably grounded, connected with the lower self or a down to earth type of person, it is possible the effects may not last long, but for those who are very sensitive and may have had severe issues within their lives it can and, will possibly, create further problems. Over the years, I have seen a few people who have been taken into mental institutions for these reasons, and most of them never regained their state of well being, or returned to normality.

Some of the symptoms for involuntary awakening the Kundalini energy may be; muscle twitching, shaking, dizziness, tingling sensations throughout the body

Now It Begins

(activating the central nervous system), tinnitus, flashbacks from the past and other symptoms, which may lead to physical complaints. Emotionally, it can create; insomnia, fear, panic attacks and paranoia, it may also create joy and happiness for short intervals, but this can be unbalanced and depression may follow.

However; when the Kundalini is awakened with professional guidance or perhaps through awareness with the steady progression of meditation, pranic breathing, yoga and spiritual development, it can open the way to enlightenment of the higher self, or as some may understand, connecting with the holy spirit.

When one's Kundalini is awakened to a high level, it can be that the person may achieve great things on this earth, positive or negative, which may depend upon their previous background in life.

Throughout history, we have all seen those who have been in power and have ruled great nations over the centuries. Some of them have used their abilities wisely and altruistically and others became tyrants.

Over the years whilst travelling to various parts of India, I have come across young people who have been attracted to and joined certain religious sects; many of these were big organisations where they followed a leader, or guru, possibly with thousands of followers.

Now It Begins

I have also noticed some people after leaving their gurus in these organisations were in need of not only grounding, but help with psychological problems. Many were very confused as to where they were going in life, some of the young girls were distraught and in tears. Of course; India has a very powerful energy about it and it can suck you in and blow you out, with its poverty and the strangest things that can happen at any time. It can affect one in many different ways, especially if a person has been there for some length of time.

Where these Sects or large groups with their leaders are concerned, there is no doubt that good intentions are present when it comes to raising one's level of awareness and spiritual energy. However; if a person is not ready for the awakening which is usually maintained in a disciplined way, especially when raising the Kundalini and being in a strange country away from home, this can create severe problems. There was once an Indian guy who had a small shop in one of the states of India near where I was staying. The banner which hung over the front of his shop read; 'Spiritual De-Busting'! At the time, I thought it was quite amusing until I saw some of his clients. He was not a very friendly type of character, in fact; he was quite hostile and the approach he used was aggressive and hostile. Apparently, from what I heard from the locals and those who I knew, he did a great job by bringing some of these spaced out and confused young people back down to earth before they returned to their home country.

Now It Begins

It is not necessary to become part of an organisation to gain spiritual progress. We all have our own path and 'You'; are your own guru. If anyone should tell you different, they are then possibly, using their powers for control. Of course; we all have choice.

Listen to others, filter the knowledge and make your own opinion, better still, just observe.

When tuning into our higher self it may not always be an easy journey as we are opening doors towards new beginnings. Obstacles may cross our path as we journey to the higher self. Do not give up; these are there to see how determined you really are in achieving the things you may truly want in your life.

The greater the obstacle the more your strength will be in overcoming them, and even though there will always be obstacles and things which may hold us back from time to time in life, as you increase your clarity about knowing yourself and where you are going in life, those obstacles will lessen, eventually having little or no effect in your life.

The only thing that prevents us from reaching our higher self in the progress of our spiritual development is the deep rooted attachments we form within our lives. When there is clarity and quietness from within, the higher and the lower soul will communicate with each other. Until that time, there is separation with little contact.

I Am

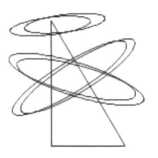

Now It Begins

I Am

Is there a path of destiny determined by fate which lies ahead for each of us, one that has been created and mapped out to follow? Or, do we make our own destiny because the path has not been laid out yet? This has puzzled humans for a long time.

Most of us do have choice, having been given the right to choose any direction in our lives, and as we continue our journey through life, the path unfolds whether it has existed or not, beforehand. Yet, we may also be treading a path which is of an eternal karmic journey and until we learn by not repeating the same mistakes in life we will continue, this is the law of cause and effect of the past, present and future.

Of course; there may well also be a greater power or source which has the final say and controls the outcome for our future disposition.

So as we make the effort with intention, we are then guided on the path of our destiny which opens and unfolds to wherever it may lead us. There is no right or wrong path for you to choose, as the one you have chosen is correct for you at the time, so that you may learn in this school of life. Look within, from your heart and you will be guided, you have only forgotten and before you can learn again you must first remember.

Now It Begins

The pathway may often appear to be sometimes dark and unlit therefore; use your brightness from within to guide you, this is the awareness of the third eye. Once you begin to find your way, dim your brightness otherwise the ego will take control and you will stumble and fall. It is only you who can know the true path which exists and lies ahead.

For the majority in this world who may continue to serve the illusion, the simplest things in life will become complex.

The greatest fulfilment of the higher self that one achieves from within will appear to be boring and filled with emptiness.

The most humble and honest person will be taken advantage of.

The greatest miracles or wonders which are visible will not be seen.

So I ask you - where does the real truth lie? Yes, it can only exist from within, where one can know the true self, the; 'I am' This goes way beyond the ego, the physical body and the mind - as you are more than all of this; you are your soul and one with the cosmos.

One who knows the higher and lower soul can never be misguided.

Now It Begins

Always stay youthful in mind and explore, remain open and in the present. When those who have remained unaware become old, they will usually only talk about their past and mundane things!

Be yourself, know what you want and live your true soul purpose, know who you are.

You know yourself more than anyone, and this is where you start building and laying the foundations for your temple of your higher self. Listen to others, but do not allow yourself to lose focus or to be put off by their negativity. Know the path of your journey.

I have wandered many times in the past, sometimes lost my way through temptations and the influence of others. I have often gone around in circles and strayed from the path, but it has now brought me to know myself and even though there will always be temptations and obstacles, I have conquered most of my fears and demons within.

Every path we may choose has its own experience; and every experience has its own limitations. It is, knowing when it is time to let go, and move on. Once again, this all comes from within. Know and be honest with yourself, this is the first stage in seeking truth. When cheating or deceiving others, remember it will only be yourself who is being cheated in the end. Listen within, if it does not feel right, then, let it go. The answers lie in finding the balance, not having to

Now It Begins

struggle in the material world or with the spiritual one. This takes practise yet; they both work together as there is no separation even though they are the yin and yang, which are opposites. Everything works together; although it is through non-attachment that will free us from our past.

Know what you want but be aware; through our desires we may create suffering for ourselves and others. It is the wants that are attached to the lower self. Have good intentions in what you truly want and how you are going to achieve it. Be pure in your heart, as what you are sending out into the universe will return. With good intentions from your heart in an altruistic way, it will magnify.

However, the more aware and enlightened we may become, the less we will have need of certain desires. We are of this entire world, but it is how we take part in it that makes the difference.

Whatever it may be that you achieve, always give thanks to the universe and feel good about yourself for achieving.

If this is your wish, start by achieving something small and work towards your goal and if you feel you have failed in any way, then look at it not as a failure but simply as not the right time for that achievement. Do not put yourself down for it. Tell yourself that it is OK and try again, one step at a time, slowly.

Now It Begins

The only failure which really exists is; 'giving up'. When seeking the self, there is no competition or race, with yourself or others. When we do; it is only the ego that is taking control and competing, trying to better ourselves against another. When you move beyond this physical comfort, you will have a greater understanding of what is, as you have no need to prove to anyone, only yourself. When we learn to go beyond the ego, reaching our hearts and even touching a higher vibration, we will then know our true selves, we will know where we are going and what our 'soul' purpose may be on this earth.

We will relinquish our fears without distractions from the negativity, which may exist around us, because we will be focused on what sets us free. Yet, we can only do and achieve this by making sacrifices. Know what no longer serves your purpose anymore.

Anger, hatred and greed will always strive to exist and will continue to do so for many. As long as they feed their ego of the lower self, those who hunger for it will be fed by it. For those who are creating a new world from their hearts, they will be at peace with the oneness and the unification with others of the same vibration. They have understood the reality and fear no longer holds them back.

The seeds have already been planted for creating and building the new world. It is no longer necessary to fight and struggle within ourselves, as it is now taking shape. Those who have worked towards this; will now

Now It Begins

find the higher self and see all has changed as they awaken after laying the foundations for the new earth. Oneness and unity of unconditional love will follow. You have now seen and touched the reality of your truth.

No matter what happens within the old world, your inner strength will grow as you glow, and others will wonder what it is about you that they do not understand. As you now realise and accept the way.

I Am

One with the universal cosmic source

I am just being and remaining in the present

I am aware of the beauty of nature which surrounds me and

the silence which exists when in meditation

I am a free spirit and have come here from where the breath of life

has brought me and I shall go wherever it will take me

I am walking the path of my destiny

I am remembering who I am

I AM

So NOW IT BEGINS

With you......

Epilogue

Now It Begins

Epilogue

About Myself and Family Background

My childhood was a reasonably happy one, until around the age of twelve or thirteen when my parents separated and I became a little confused with the world. In the 1950`s my mother and grandfather became well known, starring at the top of many of the theatres throughout Great Britain with their performances for mind reading, escapology, illusionists, clairvoyance, palmistry and working with celebrities at the BBC TV and Radio.

THE GREAT

Marlo & Daughter

B.B.C.- T.V. STAGE FAME

YOUR FUTURE
IS IN YOUR
HANDS
Grandfather & Mother
1950's

Now It Begins

I grew up in Marylebone in the 1950`s and early 60`s, just off London's Edgware Road. It was like many other areas around central London at the time I was a young child. I can remember local characters who were quite Dickensian. One elderly and eccentric lady, called Queenie, wore a very large, coloured, brimmed hat, and may have been a Pearly Queen who came from the East End of London. Another old man walked the streets with a baby's pram on top of which was an old gramophone and a small dog, which often barked and howled. The old man would wind up the gramophone, drop the arm of it and the needle would cut into the hard plastic record, blaring out loud music through the cone shaped brass funnel attached to it. He would then shout out to all who might hear him 'any old iron', as he was collecting anything that would provide him with a living. I assumed he was the local rag and bone man. In the evenings, after people had returned home from work and had had their dinner, many would go to the local pub where they had a few to drink and sang songs all night, usually accompanied by a piano or a small band, until closing time.

There were many characters around like these. These people did not have much in the material sense, but it never seemed to weigh them down as it seems to do today. They just got on with life!

I lived in an apartment owned by a housing association, which was originally built for the poor in the 1930`s. I lived with my grandparents and my

Now It Begins

parents in the cramped, split-level two-bedroom home. It was far from the wealthy area it is now, with its proximity to the West End of London. The blocks of flats were very clean and my grandmother always made sure our home was too. Unlike the road opposite, where the houses were rat infested and had staircases, which were in danger of collapsing.

I remember an Asian family living in deplorable conditions in one of these houses. There were at least twelve adults and children sharing one or two rooms together in a very small part of the house. The remainder of the house was uninhabitable.

There were many other old buildings that had been bombed during the Second World War and had not been demolished, but left to rot and decay, held up with gigantic struts of wood at the sides.

I quite often used to play in an old bombed-out theatre in which I would find objects lying between the rubble such as gun ammunition cases. One boy actually found a machine gun. I think we would have known about it if it had worked!

I did not see much of my parents during my early years and it was mainly my grandmother who took care of me. My mother was working away with my grandfather and my father travelled, driving around the country. My grandmother was a spiritual, religious kind of person and loved the Salvation Army, she did not say very much but she took good care of me. My mother told me she had been in the secret service during World War One and was sent to France on a mission.

I was quite happy in those times just doing my own thing. My first school was a church school. The church being next door to the school gave me a greater sense of spirituality and of what I thought God might be from an early age.

My mother had met my father when she was fourteen years of age; they lived next door to each other in Marylebone High Street, but did not meet until years later; that issynchronicity!

Apart from the odd outbursts of frustration, my mother has always been a very spiritual person. She led quite a hard life and spent most of her years feeling guilty with life in general, unable to receive things from others, and only able to give. My mother was shown very little love during her upbringing. When she was evacuated during the war as a child, her parents never visited her. Her father was a very strong and controlling kind of person who took her out of school when she was fourteen years old and put her on the stage to continue their mindreading act, replacing her brother who had just died at the age of sixteen. Even though my mother became famous as a clairvoyant, she shunned the limelight and resented her past. She had wanted to become a nun at an early age.

Now It Begins

My grandfather was a very authoritarian kind of person with a strong temper. He was born in Edinburgh. His father was a master baker in Princes Street and his brother, James Lindsay, played football for Scotland. In his early days, he was a bare knuckle fighter. He ran away from home at the age of twelve to join the circus but left the circus behind to join the merchant navy so he could travel the world. He then joined the army in America, broke a sergeant's jaw and had to leave rather quickly. Later on, he developed his skills in escapology and palmistry, as an illusionist and mind reader, skills for which my family became well known. My grandfather was also a very good magician and a member of the Magic Circle in the UK. He claimed to have met my grandmother during the making of a silent movie.

As an escapologist, he became known as the British Houdini. As far as I know, he was one of the first to jump out of an aeroplane wearing a straight jacket with chains and locks wrapped around him! My grandfather was a champion swimmer and dared to rise to the challenges of many death defying stunts. I have a newspaper cutting of him, diving into the Lagan Lake in Belfast with the chains, locks and a straight jacket on in the icy month of February. He told the press it was one of the most daring attempts he had ever made and was close to death before escaping from the freezing cold water.

My father was a very jovial type of character, very easy going and kind. He was brought up in Surbiton,

Now It Begins

Surrey and educated at public school. It appears he came from quite a wealthy background. I believe his mother was in her early forties at the time of meeting his father who was only twenty one at the time, which was quite unheard of in those days. It was his father's side of the family which had wealth, although my father never knew his father; he must have left when he was quite young. Later on some inheritance which had been left to my father, in which I was also included, turned up although my father saw very little of it and I saw nothing.

As a child I remember seeing the 'Markwick' crest or coat of arms on silver spoons which were given to my mother by my great-aunt. Our distant family mentioned occasionally; that a well dressed gentleman, possibly in his nineties, wearing a hat, holding a cane, and sporting spats on his shoes, had been seen walking around Piccadilly popping in out of Fortnum and Mason. They believed this person to be my great-grandfather. I have also been told one of my aunts married a prince from another country. Not sure if that is true! It is possible however my ancestors did come from another country, as my father was, and I am also, of a slightly darker complexion than on my mother's side of the family.

One thing I do know is there is a large conservation area in the county of Sussex, St Leonards on Sea, near Hastings, which bears the family name of 'Markwick', with names of streets, parks &c.

Now It Begins

My father always seemed to look up to gangsters and villainous types for some reason. It might have been something to do with his height, as he was only four feet eleven inches. He always said he was dropped as a baby by a French nurse. Even the person my mother had met, before or after (not sure which) my parents separated, had a scar down his leg, given to him by the notorious London gangsters, the Kray twins, in a card game.

It was at the time when I was around nine years old when an incident occurred. My father got involved with someone called Billy, a Canadian guy, who was apparently known to be a safe blower, using explosives, he also carried a gun. I never met this man but I do remember his girlfriend staying with us, and I kept on asking my mother why his girlfriend was always plastering her face with heavy makeup first thing in the morning.

My father teamed up with Billy, and became the getaway driver for jewellery raids. I suppose my father would have been asked to do this as everyone knew he was very good with cars and had raced in Formula 3. In fact, he later owned garages.

I had no idea what was going on but one night when I was ill, possibly with the flu, I became delirious and had an hallucination. I saw two detectives standing over me as I was lying down on the couch. I was sure they had come to take me away. My family were trying to convince me they were not real.

Now It Begins

It was not long after I had had the vision, when two detectives did actually turn up with other uniformed police from the Flying Squad and searched our apartment. They were looking for Billy's gun and my father was arrested.

We had one of the few cars in the road at the time, a new Ford Zodiac. The police took it away and apparently stripped it. My father eventually served eighteen months in Norwich prison and his partner-in-crime served nine years. After his release, my father had learned his lesson and never reverted to his old life. Although, he always held a sneaking admiration for villains right up until the days before he passed away.

When my father was in prison he told my maternal grandfather to tell me I could have anything I wanted. My grandfather asked me what I would like. This would have sent any child's imagination running wild, with all kinds of things they could possibly have. I am sure mine too went wild for a while but, for some reason after thinking about it; I said in a very quiet and shy voice, "I only want one thing"…My grandfather replied in his Scottish accent; "What is it that you want?" I said; "A bible" "No, you don't understand, what do you really want?" "You can have anything. Your father has told me so" I said; "I don't want anything… just a Bible"… "What kind of Bible?" My grandfather asked. "A small one" I replied.

My grandfather took me to the stationery shop in the High Road where he always bought his paints and

Now It Begins

brushes for his art work, and told me to choose one. I stood looking at the counter and suddenly noticed four or five small pocket size bibles stacked on top of each other right in front of me. I chose the very top one, which was leather bound and white in colour with gold leaf edged pages; it felt as if it was waiting for me to choose it, as it was the last one in stock, the others were in brown and black.

When we returned home, my grandfather wrote inside it. Even though he never went to school, he had a very good hand. The inscribed words read: *'Presented to Gary Markwick by himself in 1961'*. I still have it to this day.

By the time I was twelve I went to a new, all boys' Secondary Modern school called: Rutherford. The old schools in the area had been pulled down and its purpose was to bring together the children from two boroughs. This proved to be quite disastrous, as those from the other borough, North Paddington, were a slightly rougher bunch than those from my area. They had lived in decrepit slums and were known as street kids. Many of them would skip lessons and steal from local shops returning to school with bags filled with goods to sell to the other kids. They often spent much of the year in Borstals or detention centres.

I found it almost impossible to learn anything. There were daily riots, with the kids fighting with teachers. Chairs were thrown out of windows and on the odd occasion a teacher was stabbed by a pupil. There were also gambling and protection gangs.

Now It Begins

I kept to myself, during the times when I actually attended school. My grandfather had taught me how to fight and, as a last resort, I would also retaliate reluctantly if picked on.

The school had very strict rules. It was an anachronism, a modern school with Victorian attitudes. The teachers always picked on the quiet ones. I suppose you could say a little like 'Tom Brown's School Days'. I would often get beaten with a cane on the hands or backside for forgetting my hymn book, my school cap or physical training kit in the first year, or for talking in class. Even the head boy was allowed to mete out punishments. Many of the teachers had a rack of canes, all ranging in thickness, and they would use whatever one they deemed suitable for the occasion. Some also used their gym or personal slippers. One day, a teacher became very frustrated with the class. He walked over to me and used the wooden end of the board duster to hit me several times on the head. I looked up at him in shock, as a sadistic grin on his face seemed to indicate he was enjoying himself. Not sure what I had done wrong, I think I was just sitting quietly, possibly daydreaming and not paying attention to his science lesson.

I remember one year, we were made to play football in the open playing fields outside Wormwood Scrubs prison in London. It must have been one of the worst winters on record; we were playing in a snow blizzard

Now It Begins

with thin vests and shorts and were not allowed to wear anything else. That is one way of toughening you up I guess, although it never worked with me, never did get use to the cold! The teacher, who was training us, was an ex-Royal Marine Sergeant. I had made a friend at school, who was an Indian Sikh called Singh. One day he had forgotten his gym equipment, the PE teacher stood on the stage in the assembly hall and looked down at him. He then picked the boy up from the ground level by his shoulders and held him suspended in the air and said; "Sing, Singh." As the boy looked terrified; everyone in that hall just could not stop laughing.

With all the upheavals in school and problems at home, I began to form my own world, my own reality. I would take journeys with a friend on the London buses, as the routes stretched as far as Heathrow airport. At the airport, I would climb the stairs to the top of one of the buildings and stand on the roof where visitors were allowed, and watched the planes take off. I always knew, one day, I would also travel far; at the time of writing; I have so far visited and travelled within thirty nine countries worldwide. I would also go to museums, to the Tower of London and Madam Tussaud's waxworks or anywhere I could learn and gain knowledge. I used to climb over the fence or squeeze through the exit turnstile at London Zoo without paying, but one day, a friend who was not so slim got stuck and they had to call the fire brigade to release him, which put an end to that escapade for a while!

Now It Begins

I learned very little at school. I guess my best education was at primary school where there was one teacher who took a liking to me; and she helped me in many subjects. After the age of ten, I cannot recall learning much of anything. By the time I was twelve or thirteen, I started to rebel within society. My parents had separated and I moved with my father to the suburbs in North London, on the borders of Hampstead Garden Suburb, which was a beautiful area compared to where I had lived previously

On the first day my father took me to visit the apartment before I moved in, a lady opened the door to us, in very short lingerie. After we had left, I asked who the woman was, and my father told me it was the cleaning lady. I had my suspicions at the time, and later realised it was the person he was living with, although my father never confirmed it to me. My father's girlfriend and I fought for many years until much later on when there was a better understanding of each other. I imagine I was quite difficult to deal with and she used to tell me I was fine with her, until I went to see my mother and was totally changed on my return.

I was often used as a tug of war between them and her. In later years my mother would sometimes phone me in the early hours of the morning, to ask me what was happening in their lives, and how she felt guilty about me in those past years. My mother was always a very generous person, but had issues from the past that she hadn't dealt with. My

Now It Begins

stepmother also had her problems and became an alcoholic and also developed agoraphobia which my father and I later helped her to overcome. Before she met my father, we believe she found her ex-boyfriend lying in her home after he had committed suicide.

For the first year or two, after I had moved there, things were quite exciting; my father threw parties until the early hours of the morning. I remember most of the women were drinking gin and often in tears, and the men would be on whiskey, often quite aggressive, although there were no fights at the time. I was usually the barman.

There was one fight I do recall between my father and his best friend. At the time, we were at a nightclub in Monte Carlo, Monaco, very high up in the hills. I could hear them fighting in the toilets. It was over another woman, apparently, who had come over to join us from the UK.

After we had left the club, everyone was fairly drunk, (except for me, at thirteen) and very quiet. My father told the women who were in the back of the car to shut up. It was the first time I had heard that kind of aggressive tone from him, as he usually laughed when my mother became angry. I think he was regretting hitting his best friend. We started to descend the hill at an alarming rate, with my father's friend driving at a high speed around the winding bends with no barriers to protect us from the sheer drop below. I was silent with fear as I was almost sure we were not going to make it. We did and later, thefriendship was restored.

My father's friend, Sid, was a very carefree person who never seemed to worry about anything Years later, he became the opposite and when he found out his partner was having an affair, on top of other problems, it was too much and he committed suicide by throwing himself into Regent's Park Canal.

We travelled across Europe by road, dined in fine restaurants and went to the farm in Kent which my stepmother's father owned. I helped tame a thoroughbred race horse and was the first to ride it bare back, which was a little scary as I had never ridden a horse before! We shot game; I worked a little on the farm and learned to drive. It was all quite exciting at the time.

After that, things started slowing down a little. Many times I would come home in the afternoon from school and the doors and windows would be locked. Often when I was able to get in, my stepmother would be drunk and sleeping in bed by herself or, sometimes, with two other friends who were a couple. As far as I know, there was no sexual activity going on. I believe, during this period, we were not even speaking.

The apartment would be cold and in darkness during the winter months. My father would call home just before he returned home from working at his garage,

Now ItBegins

followed by the pub, as late as ten or eleven. Sybil's friends would leave, the lights and electric fire would be switched on and she would prepare dinner, as though it was a normal household. Often, my father was too drunk to notice anything and immediately after dinner would fall asleep.

My greatest escape came when I was fourteen and my father had managed to raise the fare for me to go to Canada with my maternal grandmother to see relatives. I stayed there for three months, also visiting the USA. This period was life changing for me because I became more independent and could see a whole new world existed beyond the mayhem in which I had been living.

When I returned, I left school at the age of fifteen, and became an apprentice motor mechanic at an exclusive garage, working on celebrities' cars such as Cliff Richard, Henry Cooper, Mitch Mitchell of Jimi Hendrix's band and Cream's Ginger Baker. We even had Prince Charles's car but I was not allowed near that one. I left, not completing my apprenticeship, and had many other jobs, wandering endlessly. I was even a grave digger for a short time.

My heart was not in any of them. The only thing I was really interested in was music. Fortunately for me, the brother of Cat Stevens (now known as Yusuf Islam) lived in the apartment above. I would hear Cat playing his new songs on the piano when he came to visit on Sunday mornings. My father used to service

Now It Begins

his new car, as Cat was just waiting for the money to come through from his first single. He was a reserved kind of person who never shook hands. His brother taught me the first three chords on the guitar, which led to a greater interest in my song writing. I had the opportunity to tour and work with Lou Reed and the Velvet Underground as a roadie but at 15, I was not ready for that at the time.

Over the years, I have played music with my partner Denize, we have had bands together and both sung. In between the music, we also had businesses together. I bought, sold and part restored MG cars for a while.

Now It Begins

One year, we decided to go to Taiwan after having seen some samples of wooden gifts. When we arrived, I met with an agent to choose the goods we would have sent onto the UK. Having no idea where to sell them, we tried them out on the corner of a market in Islington and they sold quite well. A year later, we set up at a gifts' exhibition and received orders from both department stores and smaller shops.

The business lasted for around six years until a business man let us down on the finances he used to arrange for us in order to pay for production and shipping. A, recession followed and, like many, we lost everything including our home

I had started the business purely to finance my wanderlust so I was actually very glad to walk away from what proved to be a stressful business.

I have lost two properties and many material things over three recessions. I can now say I am more content than ever in knowing my true self. There is far more to life than just money, and the few true friends who I met many years ago, still remain good friends to this day.

I have learned and taught myself most things in life. I have learned the hard way which caused me strife. However, whatever I did, I have learned through my own experiences.

Now It Begins

Whatever path we may choose in life, is the right path for us at that given time. Whatever you want in life is within your capacity to achieve but remember there is always a price. Be sure you know what you really want.

Picture Credits

- About the Author - Gary Markwick, Denize Churnin.

- Eagle, Goa, India, Gary Markwick.

- The Mirror Reflection, Temple with reflection on water in Amritsar, India, Gary Markwick.

- Letting Go, Monkeys (mother and baby) in Thailand, Gary Markwick.

- Child doing Cartwheels, Goa, India, Gary Markwick.

- Fears, Worries and Anxieties, Lion photographed in Tanzania, Gary Markwick.

- Banyan Tree, Goa, India, Denize Churnin.

- Giving and Receiving, Girls begging in Mumbai, India, Denize Churnin.

- Deserve, Beach scene in Thailand, Denize Churnin.

- Contentment, Mother and baby in Tanzania, Gary Markwick.

- Contentment, Fishermen in Sri Lanka, Gary Markwick.

Now It Begins

- Belief, Man with Umbrella in Sri Lanka, Denize Churnin.

- The Esoteric and Religions, Tree in Primrose Hill, London, Denize Churnin.

- Palmistry, Gary reads Maasai's hand in Mombasa, Kenya, Denize Churnin.

- The Story of the Goddess and the Temple, Temple in Goa, India, Gary Markwick.

- Cycles of Life, Children in rippling water in Cambodia, Gary Markwick.

- Life cycle of a butterfly, Butterfly in Goa, India, Denize Churnin.

- Live your Life as you Really Mean It, Goa, 82 year old 'Savita' (7 children / 20 grandchildren), - Denize Churnin.

- Spirituality in the Holy City of Benares (Varanasi), Cremation in Nepal, Denize Churnin.

- Meditation, Gary meditating in Goa, Denize Churnin.

- I Am, Sunset in Sri Lanka, Gary Markwick.

Now It Begins

- The World – Graphics – Denize & Gary.

- Epilogue, Gary Markwick, Denize Churnin.

- About Myself and Family Background, Gary's mother and grandfather.

- About Myself and Family Background, Picture of band 'Awakening', Andrew Churnin.

- About Myself and Family Background, Children from 'Starting Point', a charity in Goa Calangute, India, Gary Markwick.

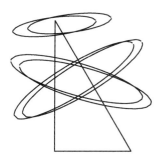

Angel channelled by Gary Markwick from Marina of Alpha Centauri - Pleiades

Visit: www.palmistryinhand.com and
www.garymarkwick.com
or email: gary@palmistryinhand.com

BV - #0059 - 150621 - C26 - 210/140/14 - PB - 9780956766885 - Gloss Lamination